Secrets of the Irish Links

Secrets of the Irish Links

A personal guide to Irish links golf, based on my 30-day, 44-course, 2,200-mile journey around the Emerald Isle

Michael Palmer

Agora Publishing, Inc.
Baltimore, Maryland

Published by Agora Inc.
14 W. Mount Vernon Place
Baltimore, MD 21201

Design by Cadie Bridges-Palmer
Photographs © Michael Palmer, unless otherwise noted

Cover Photograph: Royal Country Down Golf Club
Back Page Photograph: Strandhill Golf Club

Disclaimer: This book probably has mistakes. Check everything before you make any travel arrangements. While the author has used his best efforts to ensure the accuracy of all the information in this book, he can accept no responsibility for errors, inaccuracies, omissions, or any other inconsistency herein, or for any loss, injury, or inconvenience sustained by any traveler as a result of information or advice contained in this book. Any slights against people or organizations are unintentional. Conditions and prices change rapidly: readers should consult their travel agent as well as hotels, restaurants and golf clubs for up-to-the-minute information.

Library of Congress Cataloging-in-Publication Data
Palmer, Michael A.
Secrets of the Irish Links: A personal guide to Irish links golf, based on my 30-day, 44-course, 2,200 mile journey around the Emerald Isle
ISBN: 1-891434-31-4
1. Golf—Ireland—Guidebooks. Ireland—Guidebooks.
3. Golf—Northern Ireland—Guidebooks.

You can receive discounts on bulk purchases of this book for promotions and gifts. For more information go to: **www.irishgolfsecrets.com**

Printed in Korea

To my beautiful girls, Mary Pat and Mairéad

Acknowledgements

I need to thank a few people, without whom this book would not have been possible.

First, thanks to Mike Murphy and Mark Fost, who spent several weeks schlepping around Ireland in the cold, wind, and rain.

Thanks to all of the friendly Irish folks who were generous with their time and facilities—Frank Casey at Rosapenna, Pat O'Connor at Old Head, Phil Ferrell at Ardglass, and the nice people at Arklow, Ballybunion, and North West, in particular.

Thanks to Pat Ruddy, for reading early chapters, and for writing about his experiences building links golf courses.

A special thanks to George Rayburn and Myles Norin, who allowed me to take a month's leave to pursue this harebrained idea.

Thanks to Cadie Bridges-Palmer, my *extremely* patient and talented graphic designer.

Thanks to all of the people who have taught, mentored, and offered friendship over the years at Agora: Porter Stansberry, Steve Sjuggerud, Bill Bonner, Mark Ford, Ned Harper, Addison Wiggin, Dan Denning, Kathie Peddicord, and Nina Walters, just to name a few.

Thanks to Ryan Markish and Porter for reading early drafts and offering suggestions. Thanks to Wayne Ellis and Mike Ward for teaching me the tricks of the book trade. Thanks to Molly Ward for copyediting. Thanks to MaryBeth Wheless and Michelle Atkinson for helping to get this book printed.

Thanks Mom, Dad, and Megan for all of your support.

Finally and most importantly, thank you Mary Pat, for everything.

The Links Golf Courses of Ireland

Ballyliffin (2)
North West
Portsalon
Rosapenna (2)
St. Patrick's (2)
Dunfanaghy
Castlerock
Portstewart
Portrush (2)
Ballycastle

ATLANTIC
OCEAN

Narin &
Portnoo
Derry
NORTHERN
IRELAND

Donegal
Omagh
Belfast Airport
Belfast

Bundoran
Sligo
Strandhill
Donegal
Kirkistown

Carne
Sligo
Ardglass
Royal County Down

Enniscrone

IRELAND
Baltray
Laytown &
Bettystown
Portmarnok
Portmarnock
Hotel & Golf Link
The Island
Royal Dublin
St. Anne's

Connemara
Dublin Airport
Dublin

Galway

Aran
Islands
Lahinch
Wicklow
The European Club
Arklow

Doonbeg
Shannon Airport

Ballybunion (2)
Limerick
IRISH
SEA

Tralee
Wexford
Dingle
Waterford
Rosslare

Dooks

Killarney

Waterville
Beara
Penninsula
Cork
Cork Airport

Old Head
N
W   E
S

Mizen
Head
60 km
40 mi

Table of Contents

Introduction

The Lure of the Links

What causes a grown man with children to quit his job and build a golf course in the middle of nowhere

When you quit your job to build a golf course, most people will say you're crazy.

That's what happened to newspaperman Pat Ruddy...twice.

The first time Ruddy tried to pull this stunt, the naysayers got the last laugh. That was in 1973. Ruddy had to abandon his plan to build a course in County Sligo. The ground was wrong, and people were stealing equipment.

But Ruddy—like most Irishmen of his generation—is stubborn. He wasn't going to let the little things—like lack of money, expertise, or experience—get in his way. So he decided to try again in the 1980s.

On the lookout for a suitable site, Ruddy saw an ad in *The Irish Times* describing a stretch of earth on the country's southeast coast, about an hour's drive from Dublin. He arranged for a helicopter ride to take a look. It was perfect.

The problem was, Ruddy—again, like most working-class Irishmen his age—didn't have much money.

This was 1987. The Celtic Tiger (Ireland's amazing economic boom of the last 30 years) was just getting started. But Ruddy knew the land near Brittas Bay was too good to let slip away.

So he got a loan, re-mortgaged his home, sold his life insurance policy, and traded in his car. In short, Pat Ruddy spent every penny he had (plus lots of borrowed money too) to build a new sea-

Links courses look nothing like what you play at home. Ireland has 44 full-size links courses. Pictured here: The European Club.

side "links" golf course.

Links land, for the uninitiated, is simply the sandy terrain that connects the sea to the arable land farther inland. I'll explain more in a minute.

Friends questioned Ruddy's sanity. Family members prayed he'd give up and go back to a "real job." *But this is the lure of the links.* Pat Ruddy had been infected by the "links golf" bug, which

Links land is where the game of golf began. Everything else is just an imitation. Pictured here: Pat Ruddy's European Club.

makes a man do strange things. I read about one Los Angeles man, for example, who wanted his dead body flown 6,000 miles across the Atlantic, to be buried near the Ballybunion links. He'd visited only twice before.

Building a links golf course became an all-consuming project for Pat Ruddy. There was simply no turning back.

With literally no money to spare, Ruddy did the construction work himself, with his children's help. He actually dug the ditches, drove the tractors, and put down the grass seed and sod with his own two hands.

"I can drive every machine," Ruddy told the authors of *Links of Heaven.* "No guy can tell me a job isn't do-able on a golf course—I've done it."

As Mr. Ruddy told me recently, "It is safe to suggest that no other golf course designer's wife has spent so many hours on her knees weeding young greens. The work simply had to be done to ensure the financial future of our family. Our links required major investments, especially for a family of modest means. Simply put, we risked everything to build what we thought was a great golf course, with the hopes that the golfers would come."

Links golf, as you'll also see in this book, is like nothing you've played at home. And, as you'll also see in these pages, it does make men do strange things.

Ruddy's course took five years to build—more than twice as long as a golf course typically takes. The links finally opened in 1992.

Now, you'd think a homemade golf course built by a former newspaperman and his kids might be a quaint little links track at best, a novelty worth checking out if you happened to be passing through. But you certainly wouldn't expect to find a first-rate course by any standards.

Well... that's the amazing thing.

Pat Ruddy's European Club is simply spectacular.

The course has giant, windswept dunes, cavernous valleys, impossibly thick marram-grass rough, deep pothole bunkers (every one lined with railroad ties), incredible views of the Irish Sea, and holes that play entirely along the east coast beach.

It's no wonder *Golf Magazine* ranked three of the European Club's holes among the top 500 in the world.

And it's no wonder the world's best golfers have dropped in by helicopter to check the place out. Tiger Woods has visited (he has the course record, by the way). So have Mark O'Meara, Scott McCarron, and David Duval.

Keep in mind, this place is in the middle of nowhere. There's not another decent golf course (or hotel or restaurant, for that matter) within 30 miles.

The European Club is the kind of place where you can't wait to get to the next hole, to find out what Ruddy has in store next. It's one of the only courses in the world where you can play from the beach after an errant shot.

In short, Pat Ruddy's European Club is THE BEST golf course in all of Ireland. That's right—in a golf-crazed country with more courses per person than almost anywhere else in the world, the best course in the nation was

Links golf is full of quirky holes, like Strandhill's 13th, an extreme dogleg with a green guarded by huge mounds.

built by one man on a shoestring budget, who simply walked the land and put down the course one hole at a time. No architects, aerial photos, or computer programs involved.

How do I know this is the best golf course in Ireland?

It rains one of every three days on average in Ireland—two of every three in the Southwest. Here I hang our clothes and clubs to dry.

Because I recently spent a month traveling 2,200 miles around Ireland's coastline, visiting every seaside links golf course along the way.

I was bitten by the links bug, too.

Seven years ago, I played my first round of golf on a links course—at Lahinch, on Ireland's west coast. Ever since, I've been vowing to return, to write the ultimate guide to Ireland's links golf.

So in the fall of 2004, that's exactly what I did. I landed at Shannon Airport, drove straight to Waterville in Ireland's southwest corner, then raced clockwise back to Old Head, south of Cork. Forty-four courses in 30 days.

This was a golf adventure, not a vacation.

No museums. No shopping. No cathedrals, pub-crawls, or boat rides. We woke at the crack of dawn each morning, ate breakfast, played golf, then hopped in the car to navigate Ireland's truck-, tractor-, and sheep-filled roads to find the next links course. We typically played one course in the morning, drove 20-30 miles, and played another round in the afternoon.

At the end of the day, our clubs and clothes soaked (it rained 14 of the first 15 days), we showered... had a warm meal, then drank as much Guinness as possible before falling asleep. Then it was wake, eat, and repeat.

This book is the result of that journey.

If you are a golfer who has played Ireland's links, you know why I did it. If you are a golfer who has never been to Ireland, you won't fully understand it until you make the trip. I'm hoping this book will help convince you.

Of course, Ireland's links courses aren't the secret they were 20 years ago. Today, more than 250,000 foreigners visit the country to play golf each year.

But the good news is, many good secrets still remain.

For example, there's a course called Portsalon in County Donegal, which even most hard-core Irish links fanatics have never heard of. It costs just $40 a round, and is one of the 10 best courses in the country. There are similar bargains in County Sligo, Northern Ireland, and Dublin.

In this book, I'll tell you about many great courses you likely have never heard of. And I'll tell you how to have a golf vacation fit for a king, on a schoolteacher's budget.

What I learned during my trip was that the stories behind these courses are often as amazing as the links themselves. That's why you'll meet a whole cast of Irish characters—men who mowed the local fairways with their own lawnmowers, priests who doubled as golf course developers, Viking invaders who are buried in the middle of a fairway, and golfers who threatened their landlord with 3-irons, just to name a few.

The story of Pat Ruddy's European Club epitomizes what this book is all about—Ireland's links golf courses, and the amazing stories behind them.

I believe Ireland is, hands down, the best golf destination in the world. If you use this book, it will be impossible for you to have a bad golf trip.

I hope you benefit from it as much as I enjoyed putting it together.

Mike Palmer

Mike Palmer
Baltimore, Maryland
March 2006

It's not uncommon on links courses to have the Atlantic Ocean as a hazard. The 8th at Tralee is a good example.

1

Golf Worth Traveling 6,000 Miles to Play

You certainly don't go to Ireland for the weather.

For one, the country is as far north as Newfoundland. And it's one of the windiest places on Earth. It also rains in Ireland one out of every three days (two out of every three in the southwest).

So how can a place with such horrible weather be the best golf destination in the world, worth traveling 6,000 miles from America's West Coast, across the Atlantic to visit?

In short, you go to Ireland for the best collection of "links" golf courses on the planet.

What is a links golf course, exactly?

The word "links" actually defines the type of land. In a nutshell, links land is the sandy terrain that connects the sea to the arable land farther inland.

The term "links" comes from the Old English word "hlinc," meaning lean. And "lean" is the perfect description.

Links land is typically wind-swept, salt-laden, tree-less, and hilly. It is always close the sea, and is usually protected by giant grass-covered dunes that guard finer grasses in low-lying valleys. For newcomers, links golf courses look shockingly unfamiliar. No trees. Tremendous dunes. Tall grass. And a salty spray in the air.

Links land is sacred ground for golfers.

For centuries, this terrain was of no agricultural value, so farm-

Ireland has approximately one-third of all the links golf courses in the world, including the newest member, Doonbeg, shown here.

ers used it to graze sheep and other livestock. Animals kept the turf trimmed low. This is how it became the ideal location for golf, first played in Britain and Scotland.

Links land, in other words, is where the game of golf began several hundred years ago. Many of Ireland's great links have been around for a century or more.

Once you leave the links, as Pat Ruddy says, everything else is a toned-down copy of the original.

Like their Scottish and British counterparts, Ireland's original links were built by Mother Nature. No heavy machinery. No high-paid architects or consultants. No blueprints, irrigation systems, or computer models. The men simply put down tees and greens where Mother Nature dictated. Rabbits and sheep were the first groundskeepers. They kept the grass short, ate the weeds, and even provided fertilizer.

Links courses simply evolved—formed and molded by wind, water, shifting sand. As Geoff Shackelford says in *Grounds for Golf*, "Whether intentional or not, the early 'designers' were bona fide minimalists. They worked around what nature left behind."

Links ground is firm. Crazy bounces help bad shots and ruin good ones. A links tee shot rolls like a marble on a kitchen countertop. And then there's the wind and the rain.

After a few rounds on links courses, you will learn to like the wind. The sea breeze will clear your head. The views of the crashing waves and giant cliffs make you realize how lucky you are to be there.

On a links course, you will feel a connection to the land you've never felt before. And you will be intensely aware of your surroundings, because the playing conditions change dramatically, even during a single

Why Ireland Has Links Courses

How did links terrain come to be? Here's a very cursory overview...

Ireland and England (and the rest of the world, for that matter) were covered by glaciers 15,000 years ago, during the most recent ice age. These glaciers slowly melted, creating turbulent seas that rose and fell, and deposited lots of sand along the coastlines.

Over the next 500 or 600 years, the sea receded and, with help of the wind, pushed the sand into dune formations. These dunes were covered by plant material and bird droppings, and eventually, hearty sea grasses took hold. This is how today's links courses were created.

The southwest corner of Ireland is considered one of the oldest parts of Europe. It's probably no coincidence, then, that this area has some of the world's most dramatic links courses: Waterville, Tralee, Lahinch, and Ballybunion, to name just a few.

round. Rain. Wind. Sun. Calm. Squall. The cycle repeats.

What's great about links golf is that it's so physically and mentally demanding you will completely forget about your problems at the office or with the kids. Don't bother trying to conduct business out here either. It will take all of your concentration to simply put the tee into the ground, keep track of your ball, and get around the course without completely embarrassing yourself.

Links golf is the real deal. It allows you to play on land that has been used for golf for more than a hundred years. Links golf is the hardest golf you will ever play, but also the best by a long shot.

One reason links golf is so special—the last true links course has already been built

One reason real links golf is so special is because there isn't much of it.

Fewer than one percent of all the golf courses in the world are true links—**and almost a third of these courses are in Ireland.** The rest are scattered around Britain and Scotland, with a few in Europe and Australia.

You might think you've played a true links course before, because the

Of the thousands of golf courses in the world, fewer than one percent are true links, including Strandhill, shown here.

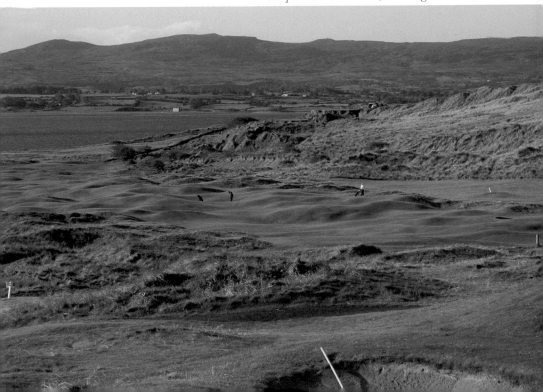

term is loosely (and mistakenly) used to describe almost every course with high grass and hilly terrain. But as golf writer Robert Frick says, "You may think you've hit the links after playing links-style courses in the United States, but that's like saying you've done Europe after visiting Epcot."

Dig beneath the surface of a links golf course and you'll find sand... all the way down to the ocean.

The truth is, there are no true links courses in the United States. In fact, there are less than 180 true links courses in the entire world. Ireland has the second largest collection, after Scotland.

We have lots of links imitations in the United States: Bandon Dunes, Pebble Beach, and Shinnecock Hills, for example. But dig beneath the surface of these courses and you will not find true links land, which is pure sand... all the way down to the sea.

For proper links golf you need porous and sandy soil. You need fescue grasses and high marram grasses in the rough. You need undulations in the form of sand dunes, which have been pushed around by wind and water. One thing you will not find is trees—they simply don't grow on real links land.

Another thing that makes links golf so special is that we're unlikely to have more than a half-dozen new links courses built in the next 50 years.

For one, coastal land is hard to come by, no matter where you go. In Ireland, like much of the rest of the world, land near the ocean costs a small fortune. And you need more than 100 acres for a full-size golf course.

Plus, scientists are finding all kinds of rare plant and animal species that inhabit the giant natural dunes characteristic of links land. Take Doonbeg Golf Course, for example, in County Clare. Here, construction was halted for more than a year because of a rare microscopic snail and because of ancient "grey" sand dunes that environmentalists wanted to protect. Today, the course's most dramatic land is permanent home to the microscopic snails and the ancient grey dunes. It's also out of bounds for golfers—guarded by an electric fence.

I wrote this book because I love links golf, and I love Ireland. What makes links golf in Ireland so special? Let me explain…

Why there are no "private" courses in Ireland

Scotland and Britain may have the most famous links golf courses in the world, but if you want to play the best 10 links golf courses in one country, Ireland is the place.

Of course, Ireland has lots of "parkland" golf courses too—more than 300 at last count. Parkland courses are just like the ones you find at home: well-manicured fairways and greens, lots of trees, lakes and ponds, etc.

But my book focuses only on Ireland's links courses. It's not that Ireland's parkland courses are bad—it's just that you can play comparable courses almost anywhere in the United States. Nowhere in the U.S. can you play a *real* links course. That's why links golf is the only kind of golf worth traveling 6,000 miles across the Atlantic to play.

And here's the amazing thing about golf in Ireland…

Even though a few courses (like Portmarnock near Dublin and Royal County Down in the north) wish to appear "exclusive," there's no such thing as a private course in this country.

In other words, every golf course is open to the public.

This gives Ireland a clear edge over Scotland and Britain, where some of the best courses remain private.

Although every course in Ireland has a membership system, every course accommodates visitors. At Lahinch, for example, roughly 25,000 non-members play the course every year. About eighty percent of these visitors are from the United States.

In Ireland, as long as you can pay the fee,

Portmarnock is one of the most exclusive golf clubs in Ireland, but you can play it even if you've only played public courses at home.

you can play every single course in the country. Imagine being able to play the best courses in America—Augusta National, Oakmont, Winged Foot. Odds are, unless you have a lot of money, or a rich and well-connected uncle, you'll never even get onto the grounds of these places.

But in Ireland, you can play the best of the best. As Pat Ruddy, Ireland's best golf architect, says, "The Irish still view golf as a game of the people. We don't view it as a business opportunity or a game of the elite. We view it as a game that can be played by all, the rich alongside the poor."

How Irish golf is different

You'll realize during your first round that Irish golf is different than what you are used to playing at home. There's a reverence for history, for tradition, and for following the rules—none of which count for much in American golf. To use a golf cart at Portmarnock Golf Club, for example, which is near Dublin and is one of the oldest and most famous links in the country, you actually have to present a note from your doctor.

If you wear shorts at Royal Portrush Golf Club in the North, you have to wear the old-school, Bermuda-style, knee-high socks. No joke.

Irish golf has no "gimmees." No mulligans. No beer-cart girls (there are a few exceptions). No stopping for a chilidog after nine holes. No whining… or club slamming. And no quitting simply because of bad weather.

Irish golf is a much faster game than the American version too.

The average round here will take you less than four hours. No lining up putts from three different angles. No half-dozen practice swings. Get to your ball, select your club, and get on with it. Be ready to hit when it's your turn. You will come to love this faster pace, I promise.

The explanation for fast play is simple. In Ireland, it rains more often than not. You want to play fast, because when it's rainy and windy, the last thing you want to do is dilly-dally around the course.

Ireland is also famous for its charming people. I know… every country claims to have friendly people. But when was the last time you called a golf course and were told you'd have a cart and scorecard waiting for you the next morning, in case you arrived before the employees? When was the last time you were told you could play your round of golf first, and simply settle up at the end of the day? When was the last time the owner of your hotel agreed to get up to serve breakfast an hour earlier than normal, just so you could have a hot meal and coffee before hitting the road? These things rarely happen to me in America, or anywhere else for that matter. But in Ireland they are not at all unusual.

Of course, Ireland (and Irish golf) is not the secret it was 15 years ago. But, as you'll see in this book, undiscovered Ireland still exists. And the nice thing about playing links courses is that they are almost all located on the coast, near small towns. Small-town Ireland is still very much the same as it was a decade ago. Men, women, and children all love to socialize. They love to play sports...to sing and dance. They love to entertain visitors, and will literally go miles out of their way to make sure you have a good time.

That's why I love links golf... and Irish links golf in particular. Which links golf courses should you play? That's what this book is all about...

What to expect from this book

In the first part of this book, I'll explain a little bit about how Ireland and Irish golf have evolved over the past hundred years. Don't worry, this is not a history lesson. You'll have just enough information, after a 10-minute read, to engage in a barstool argument.

Next, I'll give you my ranking of every links course in the country, top

Even the most exclusive courses in the country, such as Royal County Down, are open to the public.

to bottom. I've given each course a 1-100 score. Then I'll tell you what's interesting about each course—I've grouped them by region (Southwest, Northwest, North, and East). That's how it makes sense to plan your vacation. Later in this guide, I'll also give you my suggested itineraries. I'll tell you where to go on your first trip...how to play all of Ireland's great courses in a single trip...and how to take a links golf vacation on a tight budget.

Next, I'll reveal the secrets I learned on my trip. You'll learn how to save a lot of money on a rental car...what to bring and what to leave at home...how to save 50% off the rates on some courses... and how to bet like the Irish, just to name a few. I'll also reveal the 10 best bargains in Irish links golf...the 10 best links courses you've probably never heard of...the five most over-priced courses, and more.

Finally, I've included a chapter from Pat Ruddy, Ireland's greatest living golf architect, and master of the modern links. He explains what makes links golf special, how he builds a links course, and lists his top-20 Irish links. Also in this section, I've included the golf course ranking from well-known publications such as *Golf Digest* and *Golf* magazine.

A NOTE ABOUT PRICES: Golf prices in Ireland have skyrocketed in the past decade—up by 200% or more. As of publication, 1 euro was equal to $1.21, and 1 British pound was equal to $1.77.

Irish golf is no longer the secret it once was—more than 250,000 golfers visit each year. But a good number of secrets still remain, such as Strandhill Golf Club, pictured here.

2

A Short History of Golf in Ireland

Plus, how the country went from one of the poorest nations in the Western world to one of the richest

To appreciate golf in Ireland, you have to understand a little about what happened, both on and off the golf courses, over the past hundred years.

As the *Economist* reported in 2004: "Surely no other country in the rich world has seen its image change so fast."

Here are the essentials, everything you need to know to get by in a barstool argument with an Irishman.

In short, British aristocrats and the British military, who kicked local peasants from their own land, started golf in Ireland. The British chose the best sites in the country.

As one of my favorite travel writers, Jan Morris, says, "Snobby and racialist though the British Empire could be, it had a fine eye for landscape, and was particularly expert at pleasances." The British built extraordinary homes in spectacular locations—and the same can be said for their golf courses.

Lahinch Golf Club, for example, is one of the oldest golf courses in Ireland. It was founded in 1892 when members of the Scottish Black Watch, who were stationed in Limerick, worked with the Merchant Princess of Limerick to build a golf course nearby. Portsalon, one of Ireland's oldest golf clubs (built in 1891), was also founded by British military. A Colonel named B.J. Barton built the place with a grand hotel and a steamer ferry to carry guests to and from the train station south of the resort.

In the early days, British "gentlemen" played in waistcoats and bowties, ladies played in corsets and long dresses. Keep in mind, Ireland was firmly under British control—and had been for several hundred years, since England's civil war in the 1600s.

Back then, only the very wealthy played golf. It was a game for the privileged elite. The local (and very poor) Irish worked the courses. But they did not play golf. Irish men and women staffed the restaurants and hotels, caddied (often barefoot)... and washed dishes in clubhouse restaurants. They were never allowed to walk through the clubhouse front door.

How golf in Ireland almost disappeared

The Irish War of Independence lasted from 1916 to 1921. It even spread to the golf courses.

During the final day of a 1920 tournament at Lahinch, for example, a group of Irish Volunteer rebels stormed the clubhouse, removed the club flag, and raised an Irish flag instead. British soldiers were called in to re-hang a club flag before the rebels returned to perform the act again.

The giant sand dunes of Lahinch were also a place of hiding several months before the flag incident, when British soldiers burned much of the town in retaliation for the murder of four comrades.

When the revolution was over Britain held onto Northern Ireland, while the South became its own free state. Elected officials still took an oath to the British Empire.

Many new courses were built in the first half of the twentieth century, but the game remained a sport for the wealthy and well connected. The average Irish citizen was very poor. Golf was the last thing on an Irishman's mind.

As Tom Williams says in his book *100 Years of Rosslare,* in 1931 "Rosslare was still an elitist club, as all golf clubs were in these years. The background, profession, and address of prospective candidates were examined carefully before a name was put forward for election as a member. Those joining were, in the main, bankers, clergymen, doctors, dentists, and schoolteachers, and anyone whose standing in society was, in the opinion of the committee, in keeping with the standards of the golf club."

England was still upset with Irish independence, and waged a full-scale economic war on Ireland. (The British received over ninety-five percent of Ireland's exports, so it retained great influence.)

Irish farmers, for example, were forced to pay "annuities" to the British government—for land that was stolen from them years earlier! British tariffs increased the cost of Irish cattle imports by as much as 80%. Britain's economic war with Ireland ended in 1938, when Ireland paid a lump sum of 10 million pounds sterling to the British treasury. This excused Irish farmers from further payments. How generous.

The 1950s continued to be hard for Ireland, and for local golf courses. As Tom Williams says in his book, "Ireland in the 1950s was a sterile and non-progressive place, and those with an entrepreneurial spirit found it difficult to make headway in a very conservative social and financial environment."

Most golf clubs around the country lost money and membership. Rosslare Golf Club, for example, had just 50 paying members in 1957. Many clubs in Ireland were on the brink of bankruptcy. Many did, in fact, go out of business forever. The area in Donegal near Narin & Portnoo Golf Club was once the home of four golf courses. Today there's just one.

Ireland as a whole wasn't faring much better. Millions of people fled the country for the United States, Britain, and elsewhere. (An incredible 70 million people worldwide now claim Irish descent.)

Between 1951 and 1961, 409,000 people left the country. After this exodus, Ireland had its lowest population (2.8 million people) since the potato famine 115 years earlier (when the population was more than 8 million). Ireland also had one of the highest unemployment rates in the developed world. Year after year, the country battled Spain for the "worst economy in

Most golf courses, such as Strandhill, pictured below, were lucky to survive Ireland's difficult twentieth century.

Europe" title.

To give you an idea of the sorry state the sport of golf was in, consider this...

Eddie Hackett was by far the most prolific and famous Irish golf architect of this period. Over 30 years, he designed more than 30 courses (his best links are Waterville, Enniscrone, and Carne). Hackett never

Irish golf is much better off than it was just a decade ago. Narin & Portnoo (pictured here), finally has the money for serious renovations.

pocketed more than 10,000 Irish pounds for his work—that's for all of his courses combined. Often, he was paid absolutely nothing.

During these years, professional golf in Ireland was almost nonexistent. The best players went overseas to earn a decent living. Ireland's biggest tournament, the Irish Open, was discontinued for 22 years, beginning in the 1950s.

Ireland in the 1950s and 1960s was poor. Really poor. And what few foreigners came to the country weren't coming to play golf.

As Richard Phinney and Scott Whitley say in *Links of Heaven*, "Golf in Ireland probably hit its nadir in the 1950s. The Protestant merchants, military officers, and aristocrats who had started the game in Ireland had declined in numbers and wealth, and the sport held few attractions for the average farmer or working man."

But good times were on the horizon. Several key events in Ireland (and in the world of Irish golf) took place during this period, which would change the course of the country and its golf courses forever.

50% tax cuts… and Arnie comes to Ireland

First, some forward-thinking men were chosen for important positions in the national government. They formed a group called the Industrial Development Authority (IDA) in 1950. The group's main task was to attract foreign companies to set up factories and production centers.

They also did what every smart government should do—cut taxes and regulations, making it easy for people to start businesses.

The government enacted huge tax cuts. In 1956 export taxes were cut 50% in certain areas… and were eliminated altogether two years later.

Price controls, protectionism, and high tariffs—all of these things were slashed or completely abolished. (It's amazing more countries don't do the same—especially when you see how quickly it worked in Ireland.)

The government encouraged foreign investment and membership in the European Community. And in 1967, they passed a law making secondary education (the equivalent of high school in the United States) free for all citizens. They also guaranteed free transportation for kids in rural areas. These benefits were unheard of just a few years earlier. It paid off. In 1964 just one in four kids were in secondary schools. By 1994 the number hit 83%—an amazing transition in just 30 years.

At the same time, several prestigious golf tournaments came to Ireland. The Dunlop Masters tournament was played at Portmarnock in 1959 and 1965. And an even bigger tournament at the time, the Canada Cup, came to Portmarnock for the first time in 1960.

An estimated 60,000 fans swarmed the course to watch local favorites Harry Bradshaw and Christy O'Connor (who won the same team tournament in Mexico in 1958). Gary Player (who shot a course-record 65) and 48-year-old Sam Snead were there too. But it was a 30-year-old American named Arnold Palmer, making his first tournament appearance outside of the United States, who won the crowd over. Palmer said after the tourna-

In Ireland you'll find yourself driving down an ordinary road…when you stumble across a spectacular building such as Kylemore Abbey, which was built in 1868 and is located in Connemara.

ment, "It's the first time I've played a links course, and I've learned a lot of shots that will forever stand with me." Palmer would go on to win back-to-back British Open championships on links courses in 1961 and 1962 at Birkdale and Royal Troon.

Suddenly, golf became a popular sport in Ireland. More importantly, it became a game for the masses, instead of just the wealthy elite.

At about the same time several big golf tournaments were coming to Ireland, the man who is as responsible as any other for the country's revival, came home from America…

Irish-born Jack Mulcahy left during the country's civil war. In the United States he built a very successful engineering company and was soon quite rich. Mulcahy sold his company to pharmaceutical giant Pfizer, in exchange for about 33% of Pfizer's stock.

Mulcahy pushed Pfizer's board to open a citric acid manufacturing plant in Ireland to take advantage of tax breaks, other financial incentives, and a very cheap (plus well-educated and English-speaking) work force.

Mulcahy sat in on the company's negotiations with the Irish Development Association. And finally, the company agreed. In 1969, Pfizer set up a chemical plant in Ringaskiddy, Cork. Today the site in Ringaskiddy has three plants, including the group manufacturing the active ingredient for Viagra.

The changes in Ireland over the past 25 years are simply amazing.

The country has gone from an economic backwater to one of the

Thousands of years of ice, waves, and wind give Ireland one of the most dramatic coastlines in the world.

richest nations in the world. Before 1980, for example, some parts of the country had no phone service on Sunday afternoons. Now, there's not a man, woman, or child over the age of 10 who doesn't own a mobile phone. And today the Irish send more mobile-phone text messages than any other group of people on the planet.

Hollywood comes to Ireland

Jack Mulcahy was a local hero. And he was still very connected in the United States, where he hung out with Hollywood movie stars and gave lots of money to U.S. Republican presidential campaigns.

In 1968 Mulcahy made his own large investment in Ireland—a giant estate near Waterville, where he decided to "build the country's best golf course."

Actually, there was already a golf course in Waterville—or at least the remnants of a golf course.

Mulcahy hired the guy who would become Ireland's most famous architect, Eddie Hackett, who at the time had designed only two courses. Helping Hackett was one of Mulcahy's close friends, Claude Harmon (whose son Butch would later help make Tiger Woods the world's best golfer).

They took the original nine holes at Waterville, reworked them, and added nine more.

When the course opened in 1973, Mulcahy knew he had one of the best courses in the world, in one of the most private and beautiful settings. Waterville sits on the edge of the Iveragh Peninsula, off the Ring of Kerry.

Mulcahy brought his

Achill Island's cliffs, on the West Coast in County Mayo.

21

Hollywood friends to his new course. These were some of the biggest stars of the day: Bob Hope, Telly Savalas, Jack Lemmon.

The biggest names in golf quickly followed: Snead, Venturi, Floyd, and Player in the early days, followed a generation later by Woods, Stewart, Faldo, O'Meara, Appleby, Duval, Jansen, Els, and Furyk.

Today, the best players in the world regularly come to Ireland. Nick Faldo wanted to buy Ballyliffin, pictured here.

Jack Mulcahy's Pfizer deal was not the first to land an American company in Ireland, but it was certainly one of the most important.

As Ray MacSharry says in *Making of the Celtic Tiger*, some 450 companies negotiated new projects or expansions with the IDA in Ireland in the 1960s. GE opened two manufacturing businesses—one in Shannon, the other in Dundalk. In the 1970s Gillette, Wang, Merck, and Syntex arrived.

In 1978 the government passed a law cutting all taxes on corporate profits to 10% from 1981 to 2000.

Apple came to Ireland in 1979, and it put the country on the map in Silicon Valley. IBM, Lotus, and Microsoft all followed in the early 1980s. Then came Intel and Motorola, followed by Dell, Gateway, Compaq, and Hewlett Packard.

Today these companies employ tens of thousands of Irish and pay hundreds of millions in taxes. All came because of low and decreasing taxes (as low as 10%), government grants, a cheap and reliable work force, and an ideal location for shipping to Europe. Now Ireland is the only developed country with taxes as low as 12.5% on corporate profits.

With rates this low, the country is now a real tax haven. And U.S. companies continue to set up shop here.

A recent article in *The Wall Street Journal* detailed Microsoft's strategy to save $500 million a year in taxes by having operations in Ireland. The company pays about $300 million to the Irish government, or about $77 per

Irish citizen.

Today, Ireland sees "intellectual property" (software and drug patents, for example) as its future. It is probably the world's most successful tax haven, ahead of rivals such as Bermuda and the Cayman Islands.

And Ireland is quickly becoming one of the richest developed countries in the world. New houses are sprouting up everywhere. Ireland built about 80,000 new houses in 2004. Britain, with 15 times as many people, built only twice as many new houses.

Today, Irish people no longer wait on you in restaurants and bars. They've all got "high-tech" jobs. The service industry is now staffed by Slovakians, Ukranians, Lithuanians, and other Eastern Europeans.

At the same time Mulcahy was building his fantastic course in the southwest corner of the country, Irish golf got another boost.

Although the country was in the very early stages of the Celtic Tiger boom, there were still very few Americans who had ever heard of the now-famous golf courses. Even fewer considered coming for a golf vacation. But that was about to change....

Twenty-five years ago, no one came to Ireland to play golf. Now 250,000 visitors a year come to play. Pictured here: Rosapenna.

Tom Watson... and million-dollar golf course living

In 1970 American golf writer Herbert Warren Wind named the Old Course at Ballybunion one of the "World's Top 10." Tom Watson came for a visit in 1981, gushed about the course, and Americans and other foreigners have been flocking here ever since.

Now, of course, golf is a thriving business in Ireland. A round at Old Head Golf Links costs €250 (about $300). Rounds at Lahinch, Ballybunion, Portmarnock, Royal County Down, and dozens of other Irish courses are well over $100. These fees are up more than 100% in the past decade. Some are up 200% or more.

Golf tourism numbers have shot up too. According to the *Times of London*, Ireland had about 58,000 golf visitors in 1988. Today the Ireland Tourist Board says Ireland gets about 250,000 golfing visitors a year. Approximately 60% come from the U.K., roughly 15% to 20% from both the U.S. and continental Europe, and the remainder from the rest of the world.

Even super-exclusive and super-expensive golf course communities have come to Ireland. Doonbeg is the newest of Ireland's links courses, located in County Clare. It cost €150 million to build (Greg Norman was the designer). Membership costs $50,000, and a recent ad in *The Wall Street Journal* described suites, condos, and houses selling in the €750,000 to €1 million range.

Overall, like everything else in Ireland, the game of golf is a lot more expensive than it was just five or 10 years ago.

But the good news is that you don't have to look hard to find amazingly cheap gems. Portsalon Golf Club, in County Donegal (the Northwest) is twice the course Doonbeg will ever be. And get this—a one-year membership at Portsalon costs about $500—*that includes all green's fees.* One round costs less than $50, any day of the week.

The point is, if you know where to look, golf in Ireland is still an everyman's game. There are plenty of opportunities to play fantastic links golf, probably for much less than you pay to play at a local municipal course at home.

My goal in this book is to tell you everything you need to know.

3

The Links of Ireland, from First to Worst

This book has one purpose—to help you take a great golf vacation in Ireland.

You see, the problem with most Irish golf guidebooks is that "bad" or "overrated" links courses simply don't exist. There are just varying degrees of good and great.

I believe this happens for three reasons:

1) First, the Irish are proud people. They are used to being the underdogs. They don't like to say anything bad about their country. So they describe everything as "lovely" and "nice." Restaurants… towns… hotels… golf courses… you name it.

2) Some of Ireland's famous links courses earn high rankings in popular golf publications by reputation alone. To me, there's nothing more frustrating than making a long drive and shelling out $150 or more for a golf course that is mediocre at best. If you use this book, that will never happen to you. I'm not afraid to tell you which courses are overpriced. And which to avoid. The names on the clubhouse gates mean nothing to me.

3) As far as I know, no one has ever played all of Ireland's links courses on one trip—or even in one year. Most rankings are done by committee. And there's no way every committee member has played every course. I've personally visited every course ranked in this book. I did the whole journey in one month, so I can tell you how one course stacks up against another.

You'll notice that I did not cover every links course in the country. There are 53 links courses in all. But I had to draw the line somewhere. Some seaside courses are a mix of links and parkland. I did not include those. Some courses are all links, but are just too short to be considered full-size tracts. If a course is not at least 6,000 yards, or if it has fewer than 18 holes, I did not bother with it.

These two criteria eliminated a handful of courses, such as Seapoint, Corballis, and St. Helens. We also skipped Carton House, a new upscale course that claims to be a links, but is nowhere near the coast (they brought in tons of grass and soil).

How these courses are ranked

You'll notice throughout this book that I use something called the PMF grading system. This is my personal system. The "P" is for my name, Palmer; the "M" for Murphy; and the "F" for Fost. Murphy and Fost are the guys who helped me create the scoring system and rank every course along the way.

I scored each full-size links golf course in Ireland much like you might do with a bottle of wine. The top score possible is a 100, based on four criteria, which I describe below. I think this scoring system is the best way to help you figure out which courses to play—and which to avoid.

Of course, I have my biases. I favor links courses with dramatic elevation changes—elevated tee boxes, elevated greens, deep valleys, and high dunes. I like fairways that look like a black diamond ski slope—mounds and moguls everywhere. I don't mind uneven lies. Some golfers complain that these undulations aren't "fair." I don't care much about fair, I just want to play an exciting course—the kind I can't play at home.

For me there's no comparison between a hilly and elevated links course like Lahinch or the European Club (which are just spectacular)… and a flat links like Royal Dublin or Portmarnock. Lahinch and the European Club are far superior.

The other elements that help a course score well in my system are spectacular views of the coast, mountains, and ocean. Ireland has some of the most spectacular coastal scenery in the world. The best courses take advantage of it.

I also favor courses with deep pothole bunkers and excruciatingly high rough. On the hardest links courses, missing the fairway results in the automatic loss of a stroke and distance penalty. Some links courses don't grow the rough thick enough or deep enough. That's a deduction for me.

I like courses that have been around for a long time, but I don't care anything for reputation. As you'll see, I give some of the most revered courses rankings they've probably never seen before. And as a result, I may not be invited back.

But I do think these ratings are fair, made without bias. And I think they will help you have a great golf trip.

Remember, for the most part these courses are quite far away from one another, and any real civilization. You don't want to waste a whole day traveling to a famous course only to find out that it's not worth your time.

To me, if you're going to drive several hours and spend more than a $150 on a round of golf, the golf had better be pretty damn good.

There is one thing I want to make clear before you continue…

I am in no way an expert on golf course design or architecture. I'm only a better-than-average golfer. I never once broke 80 on my recent trip (although I've done it many times at home). I shot above 100 on more than one occasion in Ireland. I'm 35 years old and have been playing golf for almost two decades. I've lived in Ireland on two occasions, and worked in Ireland for about a year. I've also done a lot of traveling over the past decade, to more than 30 countries, from Russia to Ecuador, Spain to Mexico. The point is, I've seen the best golf courses all over the world… and I've gotten to know Ireland pretty well during my travels.

If you are looking for a book written by a technical design expert, this isn't it. If you want a pro's opinion, you're in the wrong place.

I wrote this book because I simply love Ireland and links golf. And because there's no better collection of links golf courses anywhere in the world.

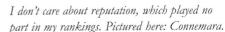

I don't care about reputation, which played no part in my rankings. Pictured here: Connemara.

Here's how the PMF ranking system works. Each course receives a ranking in four categories:

Scenery counts in my rankings. Here I hit a bunker shot at Ballybunion, just steps from the Atlantic Ocean.

1) **Design.** To me this means several things. Most importantly: Are the holes interesting? Do they offer a good variety of doglegs, elevations, length, and width? Do they make the best use of the natural terrain and scenery? Am I excited to see what the designer has in store for me next? Are the holes memorable? Are there holes that are unlike any I've ever seen before? This category counted for 30% of a course's overall score.

2) **Challenge.** This, of course, involves length and overall difficulty. But there's more to it. Does the course make you think about what to hit off the tee, or can you simply pound away with a driver on every hole? Is there more than one way to play a hole? Is it the kind of course that makes you want to play it again, to take perhaps a different approach? Are you punished for hitting bad shots? Are the greens interesting (undulated, guarded, elevated), rather than flat tabletops? This category counted for 30% of a course's overall score.

3) **Condition.** This criterium is mostly obvious: how are the greens, fairways, tee boxes, sand traps, and rough? Keep in mind, however, that links golf is not like parkland golf. The fairways will always have some bare patches… and the ground will always be a little firmer than what you are used to in the United States. This category counted for 20% of a course's overall score.

4) **19th Hole.** This score involves not only the clubhouse, but also the locker rooms, pro shop, and restaurant. This score also takes into

account the overall experience. What are the starters and pros like? How friendly is the welcome? Do the employees treat you like you don't belong or welcome you with open arms? This category counted for 20% of a course's overall score.

First-to-worst rankings of every full-size links course in Ireland

5 Stars, The Best of Ireland
Courses scoring 90 – 100 on the PMF Scale

The best in Ireland—worth spending a whole day traveling to play. Worth planning an entire vacation around. Worth playing twice.

1. The European Club	96	6. Portsalon	92
2. Waterville	95	7. Rosapenna (Sandy Hills)	92
3. Tralee	95	8. Portstewart	91
4. Old Head	94	9. Royal County Down	91
5. Lahinch	93	10. The Island	90

4 Stars, Close to the Best
Courses scoring 80 – 89 on the PMF Scale

Just short of the best—great courses by any standard, worth traveling out of your way several hours to play. You won't play anything like this at home.

11. Portrush (Dunluce)	89	16. Carne	83
12. Enniscrone	88	17. Doonbeg	83
13. Ballybunion (Old)	88	18. Dooks	82
14. Ballyliffin (Glashedy)	84	19. Portrush (Valley)	81
15. Ballybunion (Cashen)	84	20. Ballyliffin (Old)	80

3 Stars, Great Links but Something Missing
Courses scoring 70 – 79 on the PMF Scale

Great courses—but something significant is missing, which keeps these courses from the top two tiers. These courses are worth playing if you are anywhere nearby.

21. Donegal	79	26. County Louth (Baltray)	76
22. Sligo	79	27. Laytown & Bettystown	74
23. Portmarnock	78	28. Rosapenna (Tom Morris)	73
24. Narin & Portnoo	77	29. St. Anne's	72
25. Ardglass	77		

2 Stars, Good Links, but by No Means the Best
Courses Scoring 60 – 69 on the PMF Scale

Good golf courses, but not the full links experience.

30. Strandhill	69	36. Rosslare	66
31. Dingle	69	37. Portmarnock H&G	66
32. Castlerock	68	38. Royal Dublin	65
33. Connemara	68	39. Arklow	64
34-35. St. Patrick's (2 courses)	67	40. North West	61

1 Star, Bottom-Rung Links
Courses Scoring 50 – 59 on the PMF Scale

Not worth going out of your way to play.

41. Kirkistown   58
42. Dunfanaghy   57
43. Ballycastle   55
44. Bundoran   53

Membership at some of the best links in Ireland still costs less than $1,000 a year. Pictured here: Ardglass.

4

The Southwest

The links golf courses in the Southwest are more popular than those in any other region, and for good reason. The Southwest has four of the top five links courses in the country, and eight of the top 20. Of course, this area is hardly undiscovered. You will find plenty of other Americans, high prices for the best courses, and crowded conditions during the peak summer months.

My loose interpretation of the "Southwest" includes Connemara (really midwest because it's north of Galway) and Old Head (which is south of Cork City). Here are the courses in the Southwest, listed alphabetically.

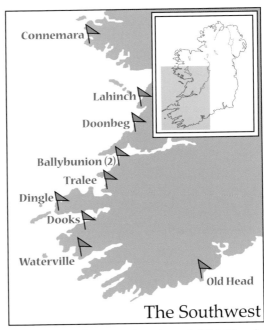

The Southwest

COURSE	PMF SCORE	PAGE
Ballybunion (Old Course)	88	32
Ballybunion (Cashen Course)	84	35
Connemara Golf Club	68	37
Dingle Golf Club	69	42
Dooks Golf Club	82	45
Doonbeg Golf Club	83	49
Lahinch Golf Club	93	54
Old Head	94	58
Tralee Golf Club	95	64
Waterville Golf Club	95	68

Ballybunion Golf Club

Old Course and Cashen Course
Founded in 1893
Ballybunion, Co. Kerry

- A local caddy's secrets drunkenly revealed...
- How Tom Watson started the Irish golfing boom...
- The best 2-course site in Ireland...and more

After about six rounds of drinks, a caddie named Liam began to tell us some of the secrets of his 24 years of working at Ballybunion. Liam explained how caddies aren't allowed to play the course or even go into the clubhouse (this is not uncommon in Ireland). He told us that Bill Clinton's statue is erected at the entrance to town because "he brokered the peace process in the North."

Liam told us about how he was a member at Ballybunion a long time ago, then left and couldn't rejoin because membership was full when he returned. We didn't know whether to believe all of Liam's tales, but the Irish never let the facts get in the way of a good story. Liam loves the golf course where he works, and is probably a great caddie.

After skipping around to a handful of bars, and exchanging rounds of drinks back and forth with Liam, we went home to rest up. We were scheduled to play both the Old Course and the newer Cashen Course at Ballybunion the next day.

One thing's for sure—it's a good thing there are pubs in Ballybunion, because there's little other reason to visit

Ballybunion's Old Course skyrocketed in popularity after a 1981 Tom Watson visit.

besides the golf.

After our first round at Ballybunion, we met another super-friendly fellow named Seamus Finnerty, for lunch. Seamus has been a member since 1965—he's now the club president. He told us about many of the famous folks who've come to play Ballybunion over the years, including Tiger Woods, Tom

You simply must hit the ball straight off the tee on links courses. Murphy was lucky to lose only one stroke here.

Watson, Ernie Els, Byron Nelson, Lee Trevino, Jack Nicklaus, Nick Faldo, Ian Woosnam, Phil Mickelson, and Greg Norman. Bill Clinton played here, and so did Dan Quayle, Tip O'Neill, Michael Jordan, Dan Marino, and Neil Armstrong.

What's amazing is that no one had ever heard of Ballybunion until an American golf writer named Herbert Warren Wind named the Old Course one of the "World's Top 10" in 1970. This inspired former USGA president

A typical day on the southwest coast of Ireland—overcast, wet, and windy as hell.

Sandy Tatum to bring Tom Watson over for a visit in 1981. It's been a favorite course for Americans ever since.

Now, Ballybunion is probably the most well-known and popular links course in the entire country.

I first saw the place when I went to the Irish Open in 2000. It's a great links course, no doubt. But for me, the course is just beneath the top tier in Ireland. I'm sure most golf writers will disagree with me, but I believe there are better, more awe-inspiring courses in Ireland that don't get half as much press.

Make no mistake about it, both Ballybunion courses are great links tests—the real deal, with high dunes, high grass, and dramatic sea views.

Although I don't rank either course in the top 10, they are both in my top 14, and they are undoubtedly the best two courses at the same site in Ireland. Of the two courses, the Old Course is more popular, more expensive, and slightly better.

I think the Cashen Course is actually harder (even though it's shorter by about 200 yards from the white tees) because of the blind shots and very difficult-to-reach greens. You'll likely lose a lot of balls on the Cashen Course if you aren't extremely accurate.

Everyone wants to play the Old Course here, but if for some reason you can play only the Cashen, don't worry, you'll still have a good time.

Although I don't put either Ballybunion course in my top 10, this is the best two-course complex in the country.

An interesting note about hole #1 on the Old Course: To the right you'll find a 300-year-old graveyard. Don't feel bad if you slice one among the centuries-old Celtic crosses. Jack Nicklaus reportedly did the same on one of his visits.

The Old Course
Founded in 1893

■ **What's good:** Great clubhouse with fantastic views… great history—most of the world's best players have played here… both courses here are among the top 14 in all of Ireland… great scenery… very welcoming and accommodating… great finishing hole, uphill dogleg left towards the clubhouse, where you can make up several strokes if you're down in a match.

The Cashen Course is in many ways harder than the Old Course—the greens are very tough to hit.

■ **What's not:** Classic but not a top-10 links… fairways were in bad condition… expensive… restricted days of play… only a handful of really inspiring and dramatic holes… there's so much hype, it's almost impossible for the course to live up to your expectations… mobile homes across from the course. Nothing to do in the town but go to a pub and play golf—but is that so bad? Course literature says they'll check your handicap certificate, but I was told there are only "occasional verification checks." You're only allowed one round per day on the Old Course.

■ **Best hole:** #11, par-4 along the ocean, three different tiers in the fairway, and high mounds on the sides… all leading to a narrow approach to the green. One of the best holes in the country.

Cashen Course
Founded in 1981, designed by Robert Trent Jones, Sr.

■ **What's good:** Dramatic elevations… you can use buggies on the Cashen Course (you can't on the Old) if you want to play a second 18 in one day.

Short course is good for those who don't hit it very far.

- **What's not:** Lots of blind drives… short for a real links challenge… greens are the hardest to hit of any in Ireland—it's very tough to score well here, even if you are hitting the ball well.

- **Best hole:** par-5 #15 with a winding, bending, switch-back fairway. It's short (only 476 yards from the white tees and 487 from the tips) reachable in two (only with two spectacular shots) but a very hard second shot. Smart play is to hit a 7-iron after a good drive to leave yourself less than 100 yards uphill to reach the green.

Ballybunion Details

Old Course PMF Score: 88

Design: 26 out of 30
Challenge: 26 out of 30
Condition: 16 out of 20
19th hole: 20 out of 20
Price: €150. You can play both courses the same day for €200.
Length: Blue: 6,598; White: 6,209
Buggies and Trolleys: Trolleys only
Tee Times: You can play any weekday… restricted times on Saturday… and not at all on Sunday. You have to pay in full at least 28 days in advance. All payments are nonrefundable and nontransferable—"unless for exceptional reasons, i.e., health," I was told.

Cashen Course PMF Score: 84

Design: 24 out of 30
Challenge: 24 out of 30
Condition: 16 out of 20
19th hole: 20 out of 20
Price: €110
Length: Blue: 6,306; White: 6,026
Buggies and Trolleys: Both
Tee times: Same as Old Course

Ballybunion Golf Club

Sandhills Road, Ballybunion,
Co. Kerry, Ireland
Tel. (353-68)27146
Fax. 27387
e-mail: bbgolfc@iol.ie
www.ballybuniongolfclub.ie

Connemara Golf Club

Founded in 1973
Ballyconneely, Co. Galway

PMF
68
Score

- Beaten to death by your own wooden leg…
- "To Hell or Connacht"—where Cromwell sent the Irish…
- An easy way to improve a unique golf setting… and more

O liver Cromwell hated the Irish. And he wanted revenge. You see, Cromwell was the leader of England beginning in 1641. He was mad at the Irish for their rebellion eight years earlier.

And Cromwell got his revenge, big time.

In 1649, he led 20,000 well-armed and well-trained British soldiers on a savage war against the Irish. He burned churches, murdered entire towns (including women and children), and, according to legend, even ordered his soldiers to beat one Irish commander to death with the man's own wooden leg.

Cromwell told Catholics they could go to "Hell or Connacht."

In other words, they were about to get a bad deal either way.

You see, Cromwell's plan was to send all Catholics to the western province of Connacht.

When you make the drive 50 miles west of Galway into this region, you'll see why. This is the rockiest, least arable land in the country.

Connemara Golf Club is located here today.

It's no mystery why Cromwell sent Irish to Connemara in the seventeenth century—the rocky soil is terrible for farming.

37

Cromwell's plan was to install his own soldiers and other Protestants on the more fertile southern, central, and eastern parts of the country. Now you can see why, when you hear the expression "To Hell or Connacht," it means you're about to get a really bad deal.

Connemara was founded by a young priest who paid a group of 10 local landowners I£50 per acre.

It's a beautiful but long drive to Connemara Golf Club. And it can be a brutal, brutal place in bad weather—rocky surfaces are wide open to the howling Atlantic winds. If you had to describe this course and this part of the country with one word, "raw" would be a good choice.

All of Ireland is known for wet and windy weather, but the courses that stick way out into the Atlantic (like Dingle and Connemara) can be really tough. We got lucky and played Connemara on about as calm a day as the place ever sees.

Connemara is a decent but not very challenging links. Of course, I say that having played it on a very calm day. It was built entirely by locals, who followed an Eddie Hackett design. I put it in the fourth tier. It's not a true links experience, but on a sunny day it does offer spectacular views from the back nine, with many elevated tees.

Like Castlerock, Connemara has a third nine (the "C" nine), which is not part of the

I told Murphy I'd give him €100 to sit on this guy's back, as we were leaving Connemara. He declined.

"championship" course. Also like Castlerock, the extra nine looks more interesting than the A and B nines. I'll play the C nine on my next visit.

What I don't understand about Connemara is how an area so famous for its rocky terrain would miss the opportunity to put these obstacles into play.

This is Connacht after all. They should have left a few of the big boulders in the fairways, used a few to guard the greens, and made a par-3 that forces you to carry a rocky surface. This is one of the few places in the world where it wouldn't be artificial.

Connemara has an interesting history. What you have to realize is that few people in this very rural and poor part of the country had ever even seen a golf course when the place was built.

Peter Waldron, a young priest who was new to the area, founded it. He arranged for the sale of the land from various owners. Eleven tenant farmers were paid I£50 an acre for their 110 acres, and one farmer with a big chunk of land got I£80 an acre for an additional 100 acres. In an 11th-hour surprise, Father Waldron had to pay a group of land speculators from Galway an additional I£8,000—the men had secretly bought up a small section of the coast where the clubhouse was being built.

Local businesses pitched in money to build the course, and townspeople bought shares of the course for I£500. Local construction crews completed

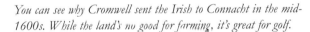

You can see why Cromwell sent the Irish to Connacht in the mid-1600s. While the land's no good for farming, it's great for golf.

the course—for a fraction of what it would normally cost.

The club was built on a shoestring budget, to say the least. Waldron hired Eddie Hackett to do the design, and when they ran out of money, Hackett worked free of charge. "Just pay me when you can," he told Walden. The golf course changed the community forever.

Only in Ireland does a priest build a golf course.

- **What's good:** Elevated tee boxes on the back nine offer spectacular views of the entire course—if you get a rare sunny day. This course is empty—you can probably show up unannounced on any day, any time of year. You'll feel good about your game when you are finished. You can spray the ball all over the place off the tee and, as long as you can find it, you'll probably have a decent approach. It's perfect for the high handicapper. Greens and fairways are in great shape.

- **What's not:** It's a long drive—about an hour and a half from Galway, in the middle of nowhere. The course is mostly flat, and wide open, with very little rough, and rocks only on the first hole. It's not a true links challenge. No high dunes and very little high grass. There's nothing else nearby whatsoever.

- **Best hole:** #18 is a 512-yard par-5 (from the whites) with a creek to carry in front of the green. You can go for it in 2. An elevated tee box encourages you

A "holiday home" near Connemara's 6th hole. Trailer parks are a common sight even near the nicest links courses.

to take a really good rip. But the best hole is one we didn't play—#7 from the C nine. It's a narrow, winding hole, with a creek that runs the length of the fairway on the left side. The green is closely guarded by large dunes.

Connemara Details

PMF Score: 68

Design: 19 out of 30
Challenge: 17 out of 30
Condition: 16 out of 20
19th Hole: 16 out of 20
Price: €60 on weekdays and weekends in high season. Cheaper otherwise—see website.
Length: Blue: 7,055 yards
White: 6,666 yards
Buggies and Trolleys: Both
Tee Times: Anytime except Sunday mornings, which are restricted to members only. Prepay full fee in advance. Cancellation policy: two weeks notice for full refund; one week for 50% refund; less than one week, no refund.

Connemara Golf Club

Ballyconneely, Clifden
Co. Galway, Ireland
Tel. (353-95) 23502
Fax. 23662
e-mail: links@iol.ie
www.connemaragolflinks.com

Dingle Golf Club

Founded in 1924
Ballyferriter, Co. Kerry

- The fungus that almost destroyed Ireland…
- A 70-year-old woman and her daughter walk 18 holes in the rain…
- The St. Andrews of Ireland?… and more

In the early 1840s, a single fungus almost wiped out an entire country. Back then, the Irish population had soared to 8 million people—nearly twice the number who live in the country today.

One of the reasons the population grew so fast was the cultivation of the potato—a near-perfect food for an agricultural society. Potatoes are full of magnesium, potassium, calcium, vitamins B and C, and iron—most of what you need to get through the day.

But Ireland's population growth changed in a hurry in 1845, when a fungus wiped out almost the entire potato crop in Ireland for several years. About a million people died during what is commonly called the "potato famine." Another million left the country by 1851.

One of the ways the government tried to help was to create "government works" projects—like ditch digging, road building, even golf course construction. The Dingle Peninsula, which is just north of the much more famous Inveragh Peninsula (where you'll find the Ring of Kerry), contains many of these famine roads and fences. You'll see them on the beautiful drive to the Dingle Golf Club, which is about as far west as you can go in Ireland.

Dingle Golf Club is also called Ceann Sibeal (its Gaelic name), pronounced "kown shibale."

The golf course is located on a tiny strip of land northwest of town. It feels like the end of the Earth… which, of course, it was for Europeans for many centuries, before exploratory journeys to the Americas.

This is one of the few places in Ireland where it feels as though little has changed in the past few decades. You are still surrounded by ring forts, burial chambers, and megalithic tombs. The western part of the peninsula is a Gaeltacht (Irish-speaking) area. Don't worry, these folks speak English too.

Golf books and magazines sometimes describe Dingle Golf Club as the "St. Andrews of Ireland." I've never played St. Andrews, but I have attended the British Open there, and I can see the connection. Both courses are relatively flat, former farmland, with many hidden burns and spectacular scenery. But the golf course terrain at both St.

Yes, you may have to stop your car for sheep and cows in the road, as we did near Dingle.

Andrews and Dingle is not at all like the spectacular Irish links courses.

Both Dingle and St. Andrews are played on rather flat, mostly uninteresting land.

I've played Dingle twice—first in 1999. The course seems harder since I played it last, although the folks running the place tell me there have been no major changes. Still, it's not a top-tier course.

As was the case in 1999, on my recent trip we had the course almost entirely to ourselves.

Here's something else you'll find only in Ireland: In the parking lot I met two women from Dublin—one in her 50s and the other in her 70s. They had driven to Dingle for the weekend and were playing (and walking) the course in a steady rain.

The Dingle Peninsula, by the way, is every bit as pretty as the more popular Ring of Kerry on the Iveragh Peninsula. And it's a lot less crowded. Mt. Brandon, on the north side of the peninsula, is Ireland's second-highest mountain (after Carrantouhill Mountain in County Kerry).

■ **What's good:** Spectacular scenery of the nearby bay and mountains... easy to get a tee time... you'll most likely have the course to yourself... great burns—classic trait for many Scottish golf links, but few Irish ones... great condition.

■ **What's not:** Pricey for a course that's not one of the best... not a very nice bar or restaurant... course is in the middle of nowhere... front nine was very flat... if you're looking for a real challenge on a typical links course, there are better options.

■ **Best hole:** #16 is a spectacular hole—by far the best on the course. It's a hole that doglegs to the right. A stream runs through the middle of the fairway just beyond tee-shot range, and runs up the right side of the green too, which is very tough to hit in any breeze. Don't be right. Bunkers guard the left. #18 is also a great finishing hole. It's long and uphill, with a third shot over a giant ridge You can barely see the flag on your approach.

Photo: Mary Pat Fannon

The Dingle Peninsula is one of the few Gaeltacht (Irish-speaking) regions in the country.

Dingle Details

PMF Score: 69

Design: 20 out of 30
Challenge: 19 out of 30
Condition: 17 out of 20
19th hole: 13 out of 20

Price: €75 on weekends during high season. Cheaper otherwise—see website.

Length: Blue: 6,737 yards
White: 6,477 yards

Buggies and Trolleys: Both

Tee Times: Payment in full in advance. If you cancel 30 days or more from your tee time, you get a full refund. Less than 30 days, 50% refund. Less than 7 days, no refund.

Dingle Golf Club

Ballyferriter, Dingle Peninsula
Co. Kerry, Ireland
Tel. (353-66) 915-6255
Fax. 915-6409
e-mail: dinglegc@iol.ie
www.dinglelinks.com

Dooks Golf Club

Founded in 1889
Glenbeigh, Co. Kerry

■ Club president threatens landlord with a 5-iron…
■ Irishwoman splits her pants on the 8th green…
■ A golf course built literally by hand, pick, and shovel… and more

"We shall man the barricades and whoever attempts to take our land will be struck down, possibly with golf clubs." That's what Dooks Golf club president Joe O'Shea told the local paper.

Mr. O'Shea was a little upset. His golf club was in a hot dispute with their absentee landlord.

Here's what happened…

Golf has been played at Dooks as far back as 1889, when officers from the Royal Horse Artillery were training at the nearby Glenbeigh Artillery Range. They introduced local aristocrats to the game.

The 9-hole club eked out an existence until the mid-1960s, when the landlord decided he was finished renting to golfers.

He told the club the 99-year lease was never officially signed, and that the golf club was closing to make way for development.

Locals began a huge smear campaign against the landlord. They held press conferences, wrote letters, and threatened a sit-in.

They even brought out the area's oldest resident: Colonel J. Hanafin. The Colonel described in a press conference how he was playing golf at Dooks way back in 1896. The landlord was vilified.

The Club tried to raise money to buy the land. They sold I£5 Development Bonds for their "Fighting Fund." After a year, they had I£2,500. They offered the landlord I£5,000, but he refused payment, and stopped collecting rent altogether.

That's when club president O'Shea threatened to take a 5-iron to anyone who tried to kick the golfers from their land.

Finally, the club and landlord agreed on a price of I£7,000, with the Irish Tourism Board picking up part of the tab.

The club decided to add nine more holes to make sure it became a proper course, so that no one would try to run them off their land again.

Over the next three years, they did exactly that. By 1970 they'd built an additional nine holes with their own hands, picks, and shovels.

The green on #13 (a 170-yard par-3 known as The Saucer), has more elevation change than any other green I've ever seen.

Here's how long-time member Declan Mangan remembers the work, according to his account in *Dooks—100 Years of Golf*:

> "I remember one fine Saturday morning, Anne my wife, my father Tadgh O'Connor and myself were working on the 8th green. At that stage a few square yards of sods had been placed in the middle of a sea of sand. Earth had been dumped at the hollow on the front right of the green, and we were transporting the earth by wheelbarrow over a pathway of planks running up to the center of the green. Anne was busy shoveling earth when disaster struck! Her elegant green slacks split right along the seam. Tadgh didn't keep his head down on the green that morning! Anne was the first lady in Dooks to come undone in one of the hazards of the new nine."

When Irish golfers first explained to me how the members owned local golf clubs, I dismissed it as quirk of local language.

But then I heard stories like the one about Dooks Golf Club, and I began to understand what these folks were talking about—and why they are so passionate about their local golf courses. Locals *really did* get together the money to buy the course, and they *really did* build the back nine with their own hands. They really *are* part-owners. No wonder they are so passionate about the place.

Dooks is a charming little course. It's not one of the best links courses in Ireland, but it does make my top 20. The main problem is that it's too short, at just over 6,400 yards. It is, on the other hand, a real links test—big elevation changes, high mounds, tough undulating greens, and some spectacular views of the Dingle Bay, Slieve Mish, the Dingle Mountains, and the McGillicudy Reeks (mountains).

This is one of the great, unpretentious places to play golf in Ireland, where you'll encounter few other tourists. When we played one Saturday morning in September, the course was crowded with locals who were trying to get in 18 holes before the All-Ireland Gaelic Football match staged later that afternoon. (Their county team—Kerry—trounced the squad from Mayo.)

The members welcomed us that morning. They handed us one of their scorecards, gave us a few pointers about the course, and sent us on our way. Try doing that at a local country club in the States where you're not a member.

It's no wonder members of Dooks love their beautiful links— they literally built the back nine with their own picks and shovels.

■ **What's good:** The history—literally built by the local members... unique holes with lots of turns and elevation... very tricky and sloped greens... elevated greens are challenging... deep bunkers will penalize you at least one shot... anything out of the fairway will also penalize you... deep rough... constant views of the Macgillicuddy Reeks and the sea.

■ **What's not:** Tee boxes aren't grown in all the way but give it time, they just built many of these new tee boxes. Many of the holes are right on top of one another—you can easily cross fairways and hit approach shots at people on other tee boxes... little short at 6,401 yards... play the tips.

■ **Best hole:** #1 was a great opening hole, which used to be even harder when the green was a hard dogleg to the left. (The secretary told me it was once the hardest opening hole in the country.) But the best hole is #13, known as the Saucer—an uphill 170-yard par-3. It seems simple enough until you get to the green. I've never seen a green with so much elevation change. If you hit it right or left of the flag, you can easily 4-putt. There's at least 6 feet of elevation change from the back of the green to the front.

Dooks Details

PMF Score: 82

Design: 25 out of 30
Challenge: 26 out of 30
Condition: 16 out of 20
19th hole: 15 out of 20
Price: €70 Mon - Sat.
    Sundays: members only
Length: White: 6,401 yards
    Yellow: 6,009 yards
Buggies and Trolleys: Both, but just one buggie for entire course.

Tee Times: Sundays are for members only; other days with restrictions. 25% deposit, 2-week notice to get refund.

Dooks Golf Club

Glenbeigh, Co. Kerry, Ireland
Tel. (353-66) 976-8205
Fax. 976-8476
e-mail: office@dooks.com
www.dooks.com

Doonbeg Golf Club

Founded in 2002
Doonbeg, Co. Clare

- The microscopic snail that cost Greg Norman millions…
- A beer-cart girl… in Ireland?
- The price of a home overlooking the 18th fairway: $1 million… and more

I t's hard to believe a snail so small you need a microscope to see it could stop construction of a multi-million dollar golf course. But that's exactly what happened in County Clare, near a town called Doonbeg. Here's the full story…

In the mid-1990s, the government-run Shannon Development Agency bought options on about 380 acres of links land near Doonbeg, about a 30-minute drive south of Lahinch.

The U.S. firm Kiawah Development Partners, who built nice courses on Kiawah Island in South Carolina, bought the options, then the land, and began work on a golf course and residential project. They hired Greg Norman to do the design—his first in Ireland.

Then, in 1999, they ran into two major problems.

First, surveyors found millions of 2 millimeter-long snails… an endangered species known as *Vertigo angustoir.* Yes, you read that right… the snails are 2 millimeters long. You can see them only under a microscope.

Environmental groups like Friends of the Irish Environment freaked out and demanded course construction stop.

"This snail is one of the few creatures in Ireland to survive the Ice

Doonbeg could be the last golf course built on natural links land in Ireland.

49

Age, and this site is one of the most important for them in the country," said Peter Lowes, spokesman for one Irish environmental group. "Cut the grass too short and there's not enough moisture. The snail dies. Weed killers and chemical sprays must also be closely monitored."

Then Norman and company ran into a second environmental problem: ancient sand dunes. I know… I didn't realize either that there are different varieties of sand dunes. Turns out the Doonbeg site contains 51 acres of giant (and ancient) sand dunes, called "grey dunes."

These dunes, I learned, are often located far from the ocean. They are important because their pH levels are much lower than the levels of younger dunes. This means better growing conditions for plants and flowers. You'll find an incredible variety of flora in grey dunes you won't see anywhere else.

These environmental problems held up completion of Doonbeg for almost two years and must have cost the developers millions.

Today, there are large areas around the course that are off-limits, guarded by electric fences. The snails and the ancient dunes have a permanent home.

The only downside is that the links of Doonbeg are now played on the relatively flat land behind the most dramatic dunes and scenery.

If this course was instead laid out on top of and around the giant dunes, it would probably be one of the most awe-inspiring golf courses in the country. The giant dunes are that spectacular.

You'll notice right away that Doonbeg is different from most of the other links courses in Ireland. My first clue was an ad I read in *The Wall Street Journal* before leaving home. It described suites, condos, and houses that are part of the Doonbeg development. The price: $750,000 to $1 million.

Laziest caddie in Ireland watches Murphy blasting out of a 10-ft. trap. He made it.

The folks at Doonbeg told me the first 28 suites in phase I of construction were sold off-plan, pre-construction. With numbers like these, it's not hard to figure out that the developers should do fine even if the golf course never makes a dime.

Don't get me wrong—I have nothing against property developments on beautiful stretches of land. (I make a living writing ads, and I've sold millions of dollars worth of vacation property in Mexico and Central America.)

But to me the appeal of Ireland and Irish golf is the unpretentiousness. Doonbeg is like the Las Vegas of the Irish links… well polished, well manicured, but a little too manufactured and out of place. Doonbeg makes my top 20, but barely. Several of the holes are spectacular. But many are not. Plus, the whole experience lacks the charms and quirks of a typical Irish links. This is the only course in Ireland where we saw a girl driving a beer cart (on the upside… she did serve cold Guinness).

What I don't understand is why you would want to own a place here when you could buy something right up the road in the town of Lahinch for less then half the Doonbeg price and play golf year-round at a much better course. Not to mention the fact that you'd be in an Irish town, surrounded by locals instead of foreigners.

But there are certainly some people who want a place like this, who can

Microscopic snails delayed Doonbeg's construction, and moved the whole project inland. Here's one of the spectacular coastal holes, the par-3 14th.

afford overpriced sterili-
ty. One thing's for sure
about the Irish: they
much prefer new con-
struction to charming
old buildings. Of course,
that's natural in a coun-
try where no one could
afford anything "new"
for most of the past 100
years.

Doonbeg is a very nice links course—and would have been even better if more of the dunes and coastline were allowed to be used.

Doonbeg caters
mostly to Americans
and other foreigners.
Membership costs
$50,000… about 100 times what you pay at even the best links courses in
Ireland. When I spoke to the folks at Doonbeg, they told me three suites
remained unsold of the 47 units in phase II.

Doonbeg apparently cost about €150 million to build (€2.4 million of
which came from the European Union). Although Greg Norman designed
it and visited more than 20 times before it opened, I'm told he hasn't been
back since. Senator George Mitchell is a member here. So are Johann
Rupert (CEO of the holding company that owns Cartier and Mount Blanc),
Wayne Huizenga (of Blockbuster fame), Jim Nantz (CBS sports anchor),

and Michael Sullivan
(former U.S. ambassa-
dor to Ireland), just to
name a few.

If these things
impress you, you'll like
Doonbeg. If you just
want to play a great
links course, and meet
some friendly local
golfers, there are better
(and cheaper) options.

Phtograhers shooting Doonbeg's 13th didn't like the flag location, so a lackey had to become a makeshift hole.

■ **What's good:** There are a few spectacular holes that play in and around the giant dunes… the greens are some of the best in the entire country—very fast and true… friendly welcome… hard-working grounds crew keeps the course in great shape.

■ **What's not:** The folks at Doonbeg take themselves a little too seriously—it's not one of the country's best courses, no matter what grading system you use… the website says 16 of 18 holes have ocean views, but that's misleading—much of the course is played on flat farmland behind the dunes. You won't find many locals playing here. Very expensive.

■ **Best hole:** #15 is a spectacular par-4 that plays along the ocean to a green that is surrounded by some of the biggest dunes on any golf course I've ever seen. #13 is also good—a par-5 with a blind tee shot.

Doonbeg Details

PMF Score: 83
Design: 23 out of 30
Challenge: 24 out of 30
Condition: 20 out of 20
19th hole: 16 out of 20
(The clubhouse was still being built when I visited.)
Price: Weekdays: €185
Weekends: €195
Length: Blue: 6,885 yards from the tips; White: 6,286
Buggies and Trolleys: Both—but, as part of one of the most ridiculous rules I've ever seen, we had to hire a caddie to drive our buggie.

Tee Times: You can play any time. You must put 10% down to reserve, and pay the balance at least 45 days in advance. If you cancel less than 30 days before your tee time, you get no refund and forfeit your deposit.

Doonbeg Golf Club
Co. Clare, Ireland
Tel. (353-65) 905-5600
Fax. 9055247
links@doonbeggolfclub.com
www.doonbeggolfclub.com

Lahinch Golf Club

Founded in 1892
Lahinch, Co. Clare

- The "bacon king" brings golf to the west coast...
- Like St. Andrews... but better?
- Goats that predict the weather... and more

I n the late 1800s, the Irish were restless under British rule. Several bad winters and a raw deal from British landlords left many Irish citizens, especially poor ones, faced with eviction and starvation.

So the Irish decided to make things difficult for the British.

Local leaders such as Charles Parnell and Michael Davitt made speeches denouncing the British. They also went to the United States for support— hundreds of thousands of Irish had emigrated to America by then. And they organized protests, attacks, and violence against the British rulers, land-lords, and aristocracy in various parts of the country.

One of these protests involved Irish workers in Mayo, who refused to help Captain Charles Boycott bring in his British lord's crops at the end of the harvest. When the Irish laborers refused to do the work, Boycott called in British loyalists and troops to help. This is where the term "boycott" comes from.

With the country sliding towards anar-chy, the British sent in the best antidote to anarchy they could find—the famous Black Watch Regiment, a group of elite soldiers from the Scottish high-lands. This regiment got their name from the dark-colored tar-

Blind tee shot at Lahinch, which was founded by members of Scotland's most elite fighting force—The Black Watch.

tans they wore… and because their main job was to "watch" the Scottish highland locals to prevent clan fighting and rebellions.

Some members of the Black Watch were stationed in Limerick, and in 1892, they worked with the Merchant Princess of Limerick to build a golf course nearby in the town of Lahinch.

This is how the game got started at one of the best golf courses in the world.

The men primarily responsible for finding the land and getting the club going were businessmen from Limerick, A.W. Shaw and R.J. Plummer. Shaw ran his family's bacon business, the second biggest in Europe, which slaughtered 150,000 pigs a year.

In 1884 the folks at Lahinch brought in Tom Morris, the world's most famous golfer at the time, who was the "Custodian of the Links" at St. Andrews, and won the British Open four times. Morris reportedly charged one pound plus travel expenses for his design.

You might hear locals describe Lahinch as the "St. Andrews of Ireland," but the truth is, the two courses look nothing alike. The comparison has more to do with the charm and history of the two courses and the Tom Morris connection (he worked at St. Andrews for more than 40 years).

While St. Andrews is very flat, Lahinch is spectacular and dramatic, with huge elevation changes, giant dunes, and deep valleys.

The green of Lahinch's most famous, completely blind, 5th hole, called The Dell.

After the train line was built between Lahinch and Dublin, the course became the most popular golf destination in the country. Remember, during these years, golf was not a game for the commoner. Not a single man or woman from the town of Lahinch was a member. Instead, it was an amusement of the rich aristocracy, royalty, and the British military. Lahinch was a course for the Protestant elite.

Today Lahinch is one of the 10 best courses in Ireland. It was redesigned by Alister Mackenzie, a Scottish doctor who quit medicine to work on some of the most famous golf courses in the world (including Cypress Point, Augusta National, and Royal Melbourne).

In recent years, Martin Hawtree completed a 5-phase redesign that has left Lahinch even better than when I played my first round here in 1999.

In short, this is one of the real classics of Irish links golf. It has everything you expect from a championship links golf course: length, blind tee shots, very high rough, dramatic ocean views, a great clubhouse, friendly people, and great history. Do not miss this course if you play golf in the Southwest.

■ **What's good:** Elevations, dramatic views, bad shots are punished… it's a tough and demanding challenge—you will be ready to put your feet up and

Some call Lahinch the St. Andrews of Ireland. The truth is, Lahinch is a much better golf course.

have a few pints when you're finished walking 18 here. Also: famous goats on the back nine reportedly predict the weather—huddled together near shelter means rain is on the way. Opening hole has a great tee box between the clubhouse and the pro shop—expect on-lookers. Blind-shot holes #4 and #5 are two of the most famous in Ireland. The South of Ireland Amateur Open Championship has been played here every year since 1895.

- **What's not:** For the average American golfer Lahinch is very tough. You need to hit the ball straight and fairly long. And you need a good short game to be able to score well here. But if you like links golf, this is a place you definitely don't want to miss.

- **Best hole:** It's a two-hole stretch: The short par-5 Klondyke #4, in which you have to hit your second shot (blind) over a huge dune. You can reach the green in two. Then there's the famous totally-blind par-3 #5 Dell hole. You hit your tee shot over a high dune to a green that is almost completely hidden. A white stone marks the line. Neither of these holes is hard—but the blind shots are unique.

Lahinch Details

PMF Score: 93
Design: 28 out of 30
Challenge: 28 out of 30
Condition: 18 out of 20
19th hole: 19 out of 20
Price: €145 year round
Length: Blue: 6,950 yards
White: 6,613 yards
Buggies and Trolleys: Trolleys and caddies, no buggies.
Tee Times: 50% nonrefundable deposit. Balance due 30 days in advance. Refunds only in an emergency. Handicap limit: 24 for men; 32 for women.

Lahinch Golf Club
Lahinch, Co. Clare, Ireland
Tel. (353-65) 708-1003
Fax. 708-1592
e-mail: info@lahinchgolf.com
www.lahinchgolf.com

Old Head Golf Club

Founded in 1997
Kinsale, Co. Cork

PMF
94
Score

- ■ $250,000 tractor falls off cliff into Atlantic…
- ■ The best clubhouse view in the world…
- ■ Shipwrecks near the fairway… and more

H aulie was too close to the 200-foot cliff. This was the mid-1990s. And Haulie was a construction worker operating a tractor on the Old Head Peninsula.

It was a cloudy and foggy day, typical for the area. On the northern-most part of the peninsula, near what would eventually become the 15th tee, Haulie was moving earth. Then, at the most inopportune time, the ground beneath the tractor gave way.

Haulie tried to reverse, but it was too late. The tractor plunged toward the Atlantic, 200 feet below. It happened in a matter of seconds.

On the way down, Haulie somehow managed to free himself from the falling vehicle. He escaped, rolled, and came away with only minor scratches. According to the version of the story I heard, Haulie left the job site that day and was never seen again. The $250,000 tractor, meanwhile, still rests at the bottom of the Atlantic.

The construction crew continued on, minus one tractor and one tractor operator. As a result of their work, this historic peninsula, with its dramatic cliffs and incredible views, is the site of one of the most unusual and spectacu-lar golf courses in the world: The Links of Old Head.

To say that The Links

Pat O'Connor, who with his brother owns Old Head Golf Club.

of Old Head is a dramatic golf course is like calling a young Bridget Bardot sexy—it's a serious understatement.

If there's a more scenic golf course anywhere in the world, I've yet to see it, even in photos. Maybe Cape Kidnappers in New Zealand. In short, Old Head is laid out on a 220-acre promontory, which juts two miles into the Atlantic. From an aerial photograph, the land that makes up the golf course looks like a giant lamb chop, surrounded by violent sea on all sides.

At Old Head you are surrounded by water on just about every hole, and the cliffs to the Atlantic are as much as 300 feet above the sea in some places.

Nine of the 18 holes play right on the cliff edges, and you can see the ocean from every hole. It's windy as hell almost every day—and can be a very tough course, almost unplayable in brutal weather.

As the *Los Angeles Times* recently wrote: "The wind blows so hard that trees could not survive."

People come expecting an Irish version of Pebble Beach, but Old Head is like Pebble Beach on steroids. Everything is extreme at Old Head—the wind, the ocean, the views, the turf, the swells, the fog, and yes, the prices.

I've played Old Head twice, most recently on a fairly calm day (15 mph winds). I played with one of the owners, Pat O'Connor—a friendly and accommodating fellow who loves history and the local wildlife. Pat and his brother John make a living developing real estate. If this isn't their most valuable property, it sure is the most interesting.

The O'Connor brothers bought this land in 1990 and opened the course for play in 1997. They got in at a good time, because it's hard to imagine the Irish government allowing this course to be built today. Luckily for you and me, the O'Connors finished the course during a time when the government was more concerned about development than conservation.

Pat O'Connor told me lots of great stories

Old Head must be one of the most spectacular golf courses in the world—nine holes play right along the cliffs.

about the course, including one about a group of Germans who got stuck on the course in a serious fog, and had to be rescued by the guys in the pro shop. And another one about a Frenchman who, during course construction, got the lighthouse keeper's wife pregnant and had to skip town when the husband found out.

Old Head Golf Links has so many great things going for it…

The scenery, of course, is incredible. It really is hard to concentrate on your golf game with so much going on around you. Watch the giant waves roll in and crash against the rocks. In really bad storms, the ocean spray can cover the whole course, which is why they've had to develop new hybrid grasses that are salt-water tolerant.

Old Head has great history—not the course itself, but this piece of land. You'll see a black-and-white-striped lighthouse built in 1853… and the ruins of a lighthouse and military observation post built a century earlier.

The promontory has seen its share of shipwrecks and tragedies. About 10 miles from shore, for example, a U-20 German submarine torpedoed the RMS *Lusitania*, and propelled the United States into World War I (see the sidebar on page 62).

Near the entrance to Old Head there's a bird sanctuary for gannets, kittiwakes, buille-

When Ireland was South of the Equator

The Old Head promontory is sandstone, formed about 350 million years ago in a shallow tropical sea. Ireland was then south of the equator. It would take another 100 million years to reach the equator, on its way up to its current latitude of 55 north.

The Old Head sandstone was already 150 million years old when the Atlantic Ocean started to open 200 million years ago, and it continues to open a fraction of an inch every year. Two hundred million years passed while a tropical coral sea covered the midlands.

Limestone formed, the land rose, rain forest developed, volcanoes erupted, deserts formed and folded, then were eroded by wind and water. The land was eventually covered by icecaps for two million years, which ground it into today's present shape. At Old Head, five caves have become tunnels, running east to west, making a bridge out of the isthmus. Out of 216 acres of land, 150 acres were farmed up to 1978. This land is now the golf course.

Whale-watching is a popular activity at Old Head. It's not uncommon to see three or more species on the same day. Look for Fin whales (70 ft and 70 tons), Sei whales, Minke whales, Orcas, Pilots, and Beaked whales. Of Ireland's 23 known whale species, 15 have been spotted here. Don't be surprised to see six species of dolphins, and porpoise too.

— Adapted, with permission, from the writings of ecologist Tom O'Byrn on the Old Head website

mots, and other rare species. Plus, the nearby town of Kinsale is one of the most attractive and inviting villages in the entire country. And it's got the best restaurants in the country, outside of the major cities.

Only 10 miles from Old Head, the RMS Lusitania *was torpedoed by the Nazis, catapulting the U.S. into World War I.*

Is this the world's best golf course? No. But it's a completely unique experience—different from anything else you will ever play. And it's located in such a spectacular setting that it's one of the few courses in the world that is actually worth the $300 price tag.

During my round, Pat O'Connor told me they are thinking about making the course more private—"sooner rather than later." Plans for 12 on-site suites under the clubhouse have already been approved. Construction will begin in 2006.

Of course, any place that charges $300 per round is already quite private. (International membership, by the way, costs $50,000, plus $2,000 annual dues.)

Pat also told me he and his brother are interested in selling off part of Old Head. (He said Donald Trump was interested… but wanted too big a share.)

When you're finished your round, save time for a few drinks in the clubhouse—it's probably the best clubhouse setting in the world. This is the one place your wife won't mind sitting for four hours while you play golf. (I know from firsthand experience.) The

This is one of the few golf courses in the world that really is worth $300 per round (not including cart fee or caddie).

view is that good.

The only downside to Old Head is that it's a course for tourists, not locals. As Pat O'Connor told a *Los Angeles Times* writer, "Locals don't play Old Head—can't afford it. It wasn't built for them anyway. It's for the international market. We have an annual day for Kinsale's police and fire—keeps 'em sweet. That's about it."

■ **What's good:** The setting, the scenery… you can't wait to see the next hole… the history of the promontory… the nearby town of Kinsale… you simply have to see Old Head to believe it… the friendly welcome… the clubhouse bar and outdoor patio. Four sets of men's tees make it easy to find a challenge that fits your game.

■ **What's not:** The price, which does not include cart or caddie fee… it's not

Old Head Disasters

The sea surrounding Old Head has been the site of many shipwrecks and sea disasters.

● On May 7, 1915, a German U-20 submarine fired two torpedoes that hit the RMS *Lusitania*, which was making her 202nd transatlantic voyage from New York to Liverpool. Of the 1,959 passengers and crew on board, 1,195 died. The boat took 15 minutes to sink and was about 11 miles from the Old Head coast.

A *Sports Illustrated* article reports that one of the ship's three salvaged propellers was bought by a company in the British Virgin Islands and forged into 3,500 sets of golf clubs.

● In dense fog in 1892, the SS *City of Chicago* (carrying 515 passengers and crew), ran full-speed into the western cliffs of Old Head. Somehow, everyone survived.

The O'Connors are making Old Head more private, raising rates, and limiting visitors. Get there soon.

really a true links land course—more like a cliffside course... the drive—Kinsale is a long way away from any other links course, and Old Head is another 30 minutes from Kinsale on very narrow roads. You won't find any locals playing here.

You're not likely to meet locals at Old Head. "Locals don't play Old Head," as Pat O'Connor says, "can't afford it."

■ **Best hole:** #12 is fantastic example of an Old Head hole. From the tee, try to cut off as much of the cliffs as possible... then you need two more straight and long shots to reach a very narrow green with the Atlantic Ocean catching anything to the left. Amazing—and a great five if you can manage it.

Old Head Details

PMF Score: 94

Design: 29 out of 30
Challenge: 29 out of 30
Condition: 16 out of 20
19th hole: 20 out of 20

Price: €250 all the time, does not include cart (€60) or caddie (€40)

Length: Black: 7,215 yards
Blue: 6,868 yards
White: 6,451 yards
Yellow: 5,550 yards

Buggies and Trolleys: Buggies and caddies, but no trolleys.

Tee Times: Full payment with credit card when you book. If you cancel more than 30 days out, you get half your money back. After that, nothing. IMPORTANT NOTE: Old Head is open only from mid-April to the end of October.

Old Head Golf Links

Kinsale, Co. Cork, Ireland
Tel. (353-21) 477-8444
Fax. 477-8022
reservations@oldheadgolf.ie
www.oldheadgolflinks.com

Tralee Golf Club

Founded in 1984
Tralee, Co. Kerry

PMF
95
Score

■ Arnie's best design?...
■ 4 shipwrecks visible from one hole...
■ 3 holes worth $200?... and more...

I n Baltimore City, where I grew up playing golf, it's not uncommon to read about golfers being held up at gun-point, or even shot. But in Ireland, it's a rarity.

One of the most famous cases occurred during the Irish Civil War (1916-1921) at Tralee Golf Club. A government soldier was enjoying some "R&R" with a relaxing game of golf. He was shot by Irish rebels right on the course. It's the only on-course murder in Ireland resulting from political violence.

Of course, it's a different scene at Tralee today.

The most danger you'll possibly find yourself in now is fighting other American tourists to get the last souvenir cap.

When we pulled into Tralee's parking lot on my recent trip, for example, two giant luxury motor coaches were in the process of unloading. Dozens of American golfers were sifting through bags, taking practice swings, and in general making a mess of the place.

You see, Tralee is unique in Ireland. It is an expensive course that attracts thousands of Americans and other foreigners every year—yet it also has a very active local membership.

The folks running Tralee are super-friendly and welcoming, especially to foreigners. They know what

A glimpse of Tralee's back nine—probably the best back nine in Ireland.

Americans want, and they've created a spectacular golf course on an incredible piece of land.

The downside of Tralee's popularity is that it's pricey… and can get crowded… and if you get stuck behind a busload of Americans (who are savoring their round with super-slow play and lots of photographs), you can find yourself in for a very long day.

Luckily, the starter hurried us off the first tee before the big group, and we had a great round.

Tralee is a fantastic golf course, no doubt. Anyone who doesn't put the place in his Irish Top 10 needs to have his head examined.

Tralee was designed by Arnold Palmer, and opened in 1984. It has everything you want in links golf—amazing scenery, huge dunes (especially on the back nine), cliff-side holes, and several opportunities to hit the ball into the Atlantic Ocean.

The back nine is famous here—and rightly so. It's probably the best nine in the country. But the front nine has recently been redesigned, and is now very good too. The front side has four or five spectacular holes, and a few that are mediocre. Number 2, for example, is a great dogleg par-5 right on the cliffs. Number 8 tempts you to hit it out over the Atlantic to shorten the hole.

I won't bore you with a play by play of every hole—just make sure you bring your best game (and your camera) for the back nine. Holes 11, 12, and 13 are as good a three-hole-stretch as any I've ever seen. Number 12 is by far the hardest hole on the course. A tremendous 40-foot chasm short and left of the green gobbles up everything but the perfect approach—which you'll likely have to hit with a 5-iron or more. Number 16 is called Shipwreck, because you can spot four sunken boats from the tee on a clear day at low tide, but also because it's a tough par-3 with no bailout area.

If you get anywhere near Tralee, play it. There are only a few courses I've played anywhere in the world that are worth more than $200 per round. Tralee is one of them. One of the nice touches at Tralee is that the caddies are members. In other words, they get to play the course. A rarity in Ireland.

The nearby beaches are beautiful. The beach right of #2 was used in scenes of the 1968 Oscar-winning movie *Ryan's Daughter*. The beach near the 15th tee is where Sir Roger Casement stepped ashore from a German submarine on Good Friday, 1916. He was arrested and hanged soon after.

To give you an idea of how far this course has come in just 20 years, the club had to organize a national raffle in the late 1980s to raise money and avoid going under. As recently as 1995, a round of golf cost only I£25-30. Now it's almost 10 times that price.

- ■ **What's good:** Back nine might be the best nine you'll ever play… condition is perfect… spectacular scenery… unique holes (giant dunes, huge bends, elevation changes, great greens, deep bunkers)… nice clubhouse and restaurant—second floor has great views of course and ocean… very attentive staff who are used to tourists and Americans… views of the beaches are unbelievable at low tide… locals get to beach on a walkway through #2… holes #11-#13 on back are worth the price alone. You can see the ocean from every hole on the course.

- ■ **What's not:** This course is well on the beaten track—don't play here if you want to avoid seeing other Americans. It's expensive, and it can get crowded. On a busy day, you can have a long round. Wide-open front nine does not punish bad shots like a traditional links course should. The front nine is more like a cliff-side course than a typical links course. Tralee closes in the winter.

- ■ **Best hole:** This is tough. Numbers 2 and 8 are fantastic on the front… so are 11, 12, 13 and 16 on the back. My vote is for #12, the hardest hole on

Tralee is a unique course—an expensive links that attracts foreigners, but has a strong local membership, and even allows caddies to play.

the course—a 458-yard par-4 from the blue tees. It's a very tough drive and an even harder second shot that must carry a 40-foot gully. It makes St. Andrews's "Valley of Sin" look like an minor ripple. My advice: If you aren't confident with your long irons, lay up on your second shot. A bogey here is a good score.

Rest up for the long walk up the steep par-5 11th, called Palmer's Peak. This begins Tralee's great 3-hole stretch.

Tralee Details

PMF Score: 95

Design: 28 out of 30
Challenge: 29 out of 30
Condition: 19 out of 20
19th hole: 19 out of 20
Price: €160 all the time
Length: Blue: 6,890 yards
White: 6,632 yards
Buggies and Trolleys: Trolleys and caddies, but no buggies.
Tee Times: Every day (with restrictions) except Sundays and bank holidays. (See holiday schedule on website.) 50% (nonrefundable) deposit required when booking. Balance due on arrival. Course is open to visitors May through October.

Tralee Golf Club

Barrow, Co. Kerry, Ireland
Tel. (353-66) 713-6379
Fax: 713-6008
e-mail: reservations@traleegolf
www.traleegolfclub.com

Waterville Golf Club

Founded in 1973
Waterville, Co. Kerry

PMF
95
Score

■ Bob Hope and Telly Savalas come to Ireland...
■ The man who saved Ireland...
■ The perfect tune-up for the Open... and more

Most of Ireland's links golf courses are the result of many locals working together. But Waterville exists because of one man: Jack Mulcahy.

Irish-born Mulcahy left for America during Ireland's Civil War (1916-1921). In the U.S. he built a successful engineering company and was soon quite rich. He sold his company to pharmaceutical giant Pfizer in exchange for about 33% of Pfizer's stock.

Mulcahy returned to Ireland in the 1950s. His plan was to enjoy a life of leisure. His love of the outdoors brought him to Waterville, known for its sea trout, salmon, bird hunting, and wild beauty.

But Mulcahy wasn't much suited for retirement.

First, he took on the task of pushing Pfizer to open a manufacturing plant in Ireland to take advantage of tax incentives and a cheap, educated work force.

Mulcahy sat in on the company's negotiations with the Irish Development Association. It paid off. In 1969, Pfizer set up a chemical plant in Ringaskiddy, Cork.

Mulcahy was a local hero. And during the negotiations with Pfizer, Mulcahy made his own large investment in Ireland. He bought a giant estate near Waterville, where he was determined to build

Waterville, in the middle of nowhere at the bottom of the Ring of Kerry, is one of the most relaxing places in all of Ireland.

the country's best golf course.

Actually, there was already a golf course in Waterville—or at least the remnants of a golf course.

Mulcahy hired the guy who would eventually become Ireland's most famous golf architect—Eddie Hackett. At the time Hackett had designed only two courses. Helping Hackett was one of Mulcahy's close friends, Claude Harmon (whose son Butch would later help make Tiger Woods the world's best golfer).

They took the original nine holes at Waterville (which were built by the men who operated the nearby transatlantic cable station), reworked them, and added a new nine.

When the course opened in 1973, Mulcahy knew he had one of the best courses in the world, located in one of the most private and beautiful settings—on the edge of the Iveragh Peninsula off the Ring of Kerry.

Mulcahy invited his Hollywood and U.S. political friends. These were the biggest stars of the day: Bob Hope, Richard Nixon, Telly Savalas, and Jack Lemmon, just to name a few.

The biggest names in golf quickly followed. First came Snead, Venturi, Floyd, and Player in the early days, then Woods, Stewart, Faldo, O'Meara,

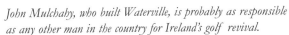

John Mulcahy, who built Waterville, is probably as responsible as any other man in the country for Ireland's golf revival.

Appleby, Duval, Jansen, Els, and Furyk in more recent years.

The best pros in the world still show up here regularly for golf vacations and to get ready for the British Open.

Mulcahy sold the course in 1987 to another group of Irish Americans. When he died, his

Waterville is a course worth building an entire vacation around. We played it on a cloudy, rainy September afternoon.

ashes were spread near the 17th hole tee box, the highest point on the course, which is named in his honor. Mulcahy gets very little recognition, but he is as responsible as any other man in the world for Ireland's golf and economic revival.

Waterville has recently undergone a three-year makeover with the help of one of the biggest names in golf architecture, Tom Fazio. (Fazio has designed seven of the top 100 courses in America according to *Golf Digest*, and was named "golf architect of the year" five years in a row by *Golf Course News*).

Five holes have been radically redesigned, and two completely new holes have been added (the 194-yard 6th and the 424-yard 7th).

With this work, Waterville is now easily one of the top three courses in the entire country. It's got everything you want in a great links course. Five holes play right along the coast, and the inland holes are filled with high dunes, incredibly difficult rough, deep bunkers, and spectacular twists and turns.

Like Tralee, The European Club, and Old Head, this is a course worth every penny... and worth building an entire vacation around.

Even with all of the great players who have visited, the course record is still a one under-par 71, by Tony Jacklin. The course record from the whites is held by the course pro, long-hitting Liam Higgins (who's still there). He shot a 65, which included a hole in one on the 364-yard par-4 16th.

Waterville is one of the hardest courses I've ever seen from the tips. You need to be a very good golfer to enjoy it at this length—7,309 yards. The whites are a much more manageable but still very challenging 6,781 yards.

Like all of the great links courses, the varying winds mean it's never the same course twice. How hard does it blow here? Manager Noel Cronin told me that on a recent visit, Tiger Woods and Mark O'Meara hit driver, pitching wedge on the 464-yard second hole the first day with the wind behind them. The next day, with the wind in their face, they hit driver, 3-wood, wedge and driver, driver, wedge, respectively. In other words, the wind changed the hole by about 250 yards.

■ **What's good:** This is an amazing layout… unique holes… great views… you get the full links experience… great clubhouse with views of three holes. It's one of the top three links in Ireland, no doubt, and I wouldn't question anyone who says it is *the* best course in the country. Redesign by Tom Fazio makes it one of the best courses in the world. If you're spending the night in the area, ask about the eighteenth-century Waterville House, a manor house owned by the same folks who own the golf course. This would be the perfect place to stay for a vacation of fishing (for Irish salmon and sea trout), hunting

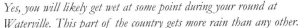

Yes, you will likely get wet at some point during your round at Waterville. This part of the country gets more rain than any other.

(for woodcock and snipe in the bogs, moors, and mountains of County Kerry), and of course, several rounds at one of the world's best golf courses.

■ **What's not:** Pricey... located at the bottom of the Ring of Kerry, which is far away from everything else. This is a very tough course for the average golfer. Don't be ashamed to play one set of tees closer than normal.

■ **Best hole:** A very tough decision, but #18 is hard to beat. It's a 593-yard (or 555 from the whites) par-5 that runs completely along the coast. The fairway has two slight twists, and the green slopes hard left towards several deep bunkers. The British publication *Golf World* named this one of the best 18 holes in Britain and Ireland.

Waterville Details

PMF Score: 95
Design: 28 out of 30
Challenge: 30 out of 30
Condition: 18 out of 20
19th hole: 19 out of 20
Price: €150 all year round (€105
    before 8am and after 4pm
    Mon. – Thurs.)
Length: Blue: 7,309 yards
    White: 6,781 yards
Buggies and Trolleys: Both

Tee Times: 25% deposit on making time... full payment due within 30 days of time... no refunds within 30 days.

Waterville Golf Links
Waterville, Co. Kerry, Ireland
Tel. (353-66) 947-4102
Fax: 947-4482
e-mail: wvgolf@iol.ie
www.watervillegolflinks.com

5

The Northwest

G olf in Ireland's Northwest region is almost as good as the Southwest—and costs a fraction of the price. A seven-day golf trip that costs $4,000 in Scotland will cost about 33% less in southwest Ireland, and about 66% less in northwest Ireland.

Two of the country's top 10 links are located here... seven of my top 20.

It was here during my recent trip that I found out "undiscovered" does still exist in the world of Irish links. This is where you'll find Ireland's best bargain, and a handful of great undiscovered courses. If you've already done the Southwest, this should be your next stop. With seven top-notch golf courses, you can play a lot of great golf without having to spend too much time on the road.

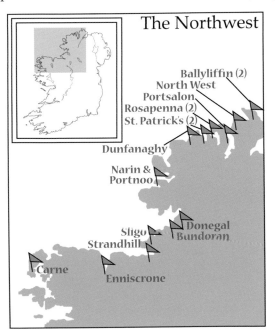

The Northwest

Ballyliffin (2)
North West
Portsalon
Rosapenna (2)
St. Patrick's (2)
Dunfanaghy
Narin & Portnoo
Sligo Donegal
Strandhill Bundoran
Carne
Enniscrone

Not only is northwest Ireland's golf less expensive than anywhere else in the country, it's also less crowded. Here are the courses listed alphabetically in the Northwest, with their corresponding PMF rankings.

COURSE	PMF SCORE	PAGE
Ballyliffin Golf Club (Old Course)	80	75
Ballyliffin (Glashedy Links Course)	84	75
Bundoran	53	80
Carne Golf Club	83	82

Donegal Gold Club	79	86
Dunfanaghy	57	89
Enniscrone Golf Club	88	93
Narin & Portnoo	77	97
North West Golf Club	61	101
Portsalon Golf Club	92	104
Rosapenna Golf Club (Sandy Hills)	92	108
Rosapenna (Old Tom Morris)	73	108
Sligo Golf Club	79	114
St. Patrick's (Maheramagorgan Links)	67	118
St. Patrick's (Tra Mor Links)	67	118
Strandhill Golf Club	69	123

* One great links course I didn't play on my trip is a little 9-hole tract called Cruit Island Golf Club, near Dungloe in County Donegal. It is extremely remote, with an unbelievable cliff-side setting. Judging from the photos and the folks I talked to on my trip, Cruit Island is easily the best 9-hole course links course in the country. Contact details: tel. (353-74) 954-3296; e-mail: cruitgc@eircom.net

Ballyliffin Golf Club

PMF 80 Old

PMF 84 Glashedy

Old Links and Glashedy Links
Founded in 1947
Ballyliffin, Co. Donegal

- Using your own mower to cut the fairways…
- Turning down Nick Faldo…
- Two great courses you can have almost completely to yourself… and more

I magine showing up for your Sunday golf match and the fairway grass is a little high. But instead of storming into the pro shop, you simply pull your lawnmower from the trunk and give the place a trim.

This is exactly what members at Ballyliffin had to do 50 years ago.

You see, in 1947, local townspeople got together and decided to build a golf course. They found 10 local landowners who were willing to lease them land for I£1 per year.

A nine-hole course soon opened for play. The members spent I£10 for one lawnmower, but it broke constantly. So before their tee times, they showed up with their own mowers to take care of the grass. They also installed and maintained wire boundaries around the greens to keep off the animals (rabbits and sheep) that patrolled the fairways.

There was no clubhouse, so they used the nearby Stratford Hotel until they could get the money for a proper building. The landowners extended the lease until the early 1970s, and the club turned a I£500 profit for the first time in 1965. When it became clear in the early 1970s that the landowners were not going to renew the lease, members organized a group to purchase roughly 400 acres from the farmers. The land was located outside of the nine original holes.

Nick Faldo liked Ballyliffin so much he offered to buy the place. The members wisely turned him down.

By 1973 there were 18 new holes (now the "Old Course"). To pay for this land and work, members bought shares in the club, with the hopes of earning a positive future return on their investment. It took a heck of a long time to pay off...

Ballyliffin is a long way from anywhere—you'll most likely have the course practically to yourself.

Throughout the 1970s, the course was in a state of constant financial crisis— racking up I£10,000 in debt in 1977 alone. Members devised one scheme after another to keep their links afloat—monthly concerts, flea markets, and raffles to name a few. But Ballyliffin Golf Club continued to struggle.

It was good fortune, really, that enabled the place to survive. Members built a new clubhouse in 1987. Then came the surge in golf popularity in Ireland and a wave of foreign tourists, the likes of which the place had never seen. Keep in mind, Ireland had only about 50,000 foreign golfing visitors in 1988; now about 250,000 people make the journey every year.

Ballyliffin got a big boost in 1993 when defending British Open champion Nick Faldo arrived by helicopter and proclaimed the Old Course the finest piece of natural links he'd ever played. In fact, Faldo liked the place so much he put an offer on it, proposing to lease the club for 33 years and to develop a new course and hotel as part of the deal. The members turned him down.

The folks at Ballyliffin decided to build another 18-hole course on their own (the Glashedy Links), which opened in 1995.

The story of Ballyliffin is yet another amazing tale of a great golf course somehow surviving decades of eco-

The view from The Stratford Hotel looking towards Ballyliffin.

nomic problems. You hear similar stories at golf clubs all over Ireland—so many clubs barely escaped shutting down entirely during Ireland's lean years.

So it's easy to understand why members are so passionate about their clubs and why they are so excited to show them off to newcomers. It also explains why they are fascinated by modern clubhouses and maintenance equipment. You can't blame them. They simply had to do without for so long.

We played both courses at Ballyliffin on a glorious Friday in early October. It was a sunny, breezy day. We saw only a few dozen other golfers during our 10 hours at the club. There was a small group of Germans playing in the morning… and we had the place mostly to ourselves in the afternoon.

After Ballybunion, Rosapenna, and Portrush, Ballyliffin is the fourth-best two-course links destination in Ireland. Both courses are great but a notch below the country's top-tier links. The Glashedy Links is supposed to

This is a beautiful part of the country—the Gap of Mamore and Malin Head, particularly.

be the "championship" links, but the Old Links is just as nice. What's interesting is the contrasting styles of the fairways on the two courses. The Glashedy Links was built with modern equipment, so the fairways are wide and relatively flat. The Old Links, however, retains all of the bumps and humps of natural links land.

This is a beautiful and almost completely unspoiled part of the country—certainly worth a trip well out of your way. The Inishowen Peninsula, Gap of Mamore, and Malin Head make the ride enjoyable. Ballyliffin is the northern-most course in country, farther north even than any of the Northern Ireland courses.

Although he didn't get the club, Nick Faldo is now involved in upgrading the Old Links—adding bunkers, moving tees, and expanding greens. The front nine is done, and the back nine will be done by the end of 2006.

■ **What's good:** This is a great place to spend a day or two. The greens on the Old and Glashedy courses were some of the nicest we played. They were fast and true, but soft enough to hold a well-struck 4- or 5-iron. Both courses are perfect links tracts for the mid-range player. Not too tough, but you get the full links experience. You can miss the fairways and still have a shot very often. We hit a lot of balls out of the fairway, but lost only one the entire round. The greens have tons of bumps and humps and elevation changes. There are elevated tees and lots of elevated holes. You could have a great golfing holiday playing just these two courses. Also: The beautiful Glashedy

*Pat Ruddy convinced the folks in Ballyliffin to build a new
18-hole course before government regulations changed.*

Rock in the distance… one of the best-stocked clubhouses in the country (with reasonable prices for all kinds of equipment and apparel)… a great place to eat and drink after your round, with spectacular views… and cheap.

- **What's not:** Not as challenging as the top-tier courses… no real spectacular holes. Ballyliffin has two very nice courses, but we heard so much hype it just didn't live up to our expectations. No holes along the coast.

- **Best hole:** Old Course: #18, a dogleg par-5 of 554 yards allows you to make up some ground on the last hole. Glashedy Links: #15, a 430-yard dogleg left with great dunes on both sides, and three tough green-side bunkers.

Ballyliffin Details

Old Course PMF Score: 80
Design: 21 out of 30
Challenge: 21 out of 30
Condition: 19 out of 20
19th hole: 19 out of 20

Glashedy Course PMF Score: 84
Design: 23 out of 30
Challenge: 23 out of 30
Condition: 19 out of 20
19th hole: 19 out of 20

Price: Old Course: €60 weekdays
€65 weekends
Glashedy Course: €70 weekdays
€80 weekends
Both on the same day: €120
Discounted winter rates November through March.

Length: Old Course whites: 6,612; yellow: 6,289
Glashedy blacks: 7,217; gold: 6,897; white: 6,464

Buggies and Trolleys: Both

Tee Times: Visitors any time. Non-refundable 25% deposit required.

Ballyliffin Golf Club
Ballyliffin, Inishowen
Co. Donegal, Ireland
Tel. (353-74) 937-6119
Fax. 937-6672
info@ballyliffingolfclub.com
www.ballyliffingolfclub.com

Bundoran Golf Club

Founded in 1894
Bundoran, Co. Donegal

PMF
53
Score

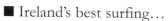

- Ireland's best surfing…
- An ideal spot to build your own links course… and more

For surfers, there's no better place in Ireland than Bundoran. Here you'll find some of the best surfing in Europe. You'll see what I mean as soon as you pull into town. You'll hear the ocean from a mile away. The views are spectacular. It's a sea of white foam… huge wave after huge wave, which is why they hold the Irish surfing championships here every year.

Unfortunately, the surfing at Bundoran is a lot better than the golf.

We didn't play the course because a ladies tournament was scheduled the day of our visit, but we walked the entire links during a brilliant sunset one evening.

This is not a classic links course by any means—no high grass or sandy dunes. You should definitely not go far out of your way to play it. It's comparable to a mediocre municipal course in the States. Nets guard tee boxes on several holes because they are so close to the previous green.

There is one really remarkable feature about Bundoran, however…

The best undeveloped links land I saw in the entire country is located just north of Bundoran Golf Club. It's spectacular, and gives you an interesting look at what the best links looks like before being molded into a golf course. If you want to build a course in Ireland, I didn't see a better spot than this. I don't know who owns it, what it would cost, or if you would even be allowed to build here. But it's where I'd start if I was in the market.

- **What's good:** The views of the tremendous surf. If you want a day where you can just rip away with the driver and play on a hangover, this course will suit. Two of the holes run along the length of the coast, with spectacular views.
- **What's not:** Not a true links experience. Mostly a flat and uninteresting layout.

It's a boring design, with almost no rough. The ground was soggier than I've ever seen links land get—probably not a true links course.

- **Best hole:** Number 15 is a 440-yard par-4 that runs along the coast with the ocean to the left the entire way. Number 8 is good too... it's uphill with the ocean to the left. Number 9 is also interesting because the green is surrounded on two sides by the Great Northern Hotel... literally 20 feet away. You could land an errant approach in a guest's suitcase.

Bundoran Details

PMF Score: 53
Design: 12 out of 30
Challenge: 14 out of 30
Condition: 14 out of 20
19th Hole: 13 out of 20
Price: €45 on weekdays
€55 on weekends.
Length: Blue: 6,256 yards
Yellow: 5,926 yards
Buggies and Trolleys: Both

Tee Times: No restrictions or deposits required.

Bundoran Golf Club
Bundoran
Co. Donegal, Ireland
Tel. (353-71) 984-1302
Fax. 984-2014
bundorangolfclub@eircom.net
www.bundorangolfclub.com

Carne Golf Links

Founded in 1992
Belmullet, Co. Mayo

- A golf course built by 27 farmers…
- The most beautiful girl in the country, in the most unlikely place…
- A good place to go for drunken arguments… and more

"Goddamn Americans." That's what a drunken Irishman mumbled in our direction while slumping from his bar stool, at about 3 o'clock in the afternoon.

In every town we visited, our first choice among B&Bs was always a place with its own bar. It makes getting to your bed that much easier.

We found one almost immediately when we arrived in Belmullet, just off the central circle that makes up the "downtown."

We went inside to see about available rooms and found two old Irishmen and a bartender (who doubled as hotel reception).

The two old men looked like they hadn't stopped drinking from the night before. Disheveled hair, clothes that hadn't been washed in a week. They spoke several decibels louder than necessary.

After one mumbled "Goddamn Americans," the other repeated over and over again how he was "just trying to be nice and buy us a drink."

Harmless drunks are still charming, especially Irish ones… and in Carne, you'll find plenty. It's no wonder. The town is about as remote as you can get in a country still full of remote locations. Belmullet is located on a peninsula, dozens of miles from any real civilization. It's like the West Virginia or western rural Oregon of Ireland. If you want to know what Ireland was like 20 years ago, look no further.

This charming place had no vacancies, so we found a B&B farther up the road, then visited almost every bar in town, before coming back to the same place I just described.

Our two friends were gone, but in the back bar there was an entertaining party of about 12 Irishwomen, out on a Thursday night for a birthday bash.

These women ordered round after round, and danced and sang all night. No matter where you go in Ireland, the women know how to party.

Here at the bar, we ran into a 50ish Irish guy who sat on my barstool when I got up to use the men's room.

Carne has some of the most dramatic dunes and elevation changes in the country. It could easily be a Top-10 course with some work.

My buddy told him the seat was taken, and the Belmullet man shot back, "You Americans think you can just claim everything, don't you?"

If you like harmless drunken arguments, the Belmullet peninsula is the place to go.

On the bright side, we also saw the most beautiful girl of our entire trip in this bar.

We were in Belmullet, of course, not to argue with drunks or stare at pretty girls, but to play golf.

We played Carne Golf Links first thing the next morning.

It was typical West Coast Irish day—a sideways drenching rain when we pulled into the parking lot, then sunny and full of spectacular rainbows several hours later.

We were the first ones to arrive at the course and waited about fifteen minutes for another car to show. Luckily it was the woman who works in the pro shop.

Carne is a very nice links course, but it's not in the top tier, even though you'll hear more people call this Ireland's "undiscovered gem" than any other course.

Belmullet was a nine-hole course built in a different location in 1925. The current course was designed by Ireland's most famous golf architect, Eddie Hackett. The course was built to promote tourism in the area and was paid for in part by the government.

Hackett loved the look of the raw land and said, "It took nature thousands of years to create this land, we must not let the bulldozer destroy it." So the course was built by 27 local farmers, who used their hand spades and rakes. They started in 1987 and finished in 1993. Some of these fellows, who had never picked up a golf club in their lives, are still at Carne today, including the greenskeeper and course foreman.

The first nine opened in 1993, the second in 1995. It was Hackett's last course, and I heard from several people that he couldn't get around very well at this point in his life (he was 77). That might be one of the reasons the course doesn't live up to his other great designs (Waterville and Enniscrone, for example). Before he died, Hackett said about his last course, "I am thrilled with the way it has turned out, and reiterate my first opinion that ultimately there will be no better links course in the country; or I doubt anywhere."

The setting for Carne is no doubt dramatic. There are huge (and I mean huge) undulating dunes, lots of blind shots, and invigorating twists and turns. It's a great links course, just not in the top tier.

If you gave Ireland's best present-day architect (Pat Ruddy) a shot at a redesign, it could easily sneak into Ireland's top 10. But it's not there yet.

American architect Jim Engh is adding a new nine to Carne, which will intermingle among the current 18 and will be completed in a few years.

■ **What's good:** This is a true links experience—high dunes and lots of elevation changes, blind shots, etc. Great scenery, with two islands (Inis Gloire and Inis

You'll actually get tired of seeing rainbows in Ireland. This was the first full one I'd ever seen—both ends "touching" the ground.

Geidhe) in the backdrop. Friendly welcome… cheap green fees… easy to get a tee time. The dunes here are simply spectacular—often twice as big as the more famous Ballybunion. The folks at Carne are set to begin work on an additional nine holes, which will open in a few years.

■ **What's not:** A little short from the white tees… you might want to play the back set. Very little to do in nearby Belmullet, and it's a long way from anywhere you want to be. No real awe-inspiring holes.

■ **Best hole:** #12 is a very short par-4 (just 330 yards) that turns 90 degrees to the left, after a short tee shot over a big mound. It's an uphill approach that can be an easy birdie… or much worse if you're too aggressive. #18 is a good par-5 finishing hole. You can see Blacksod Bay and the Atlantic Ocean from the tee. After hitting my approach, I turned to see a full rainbow. The area right of the tee is an ancient burial ground.

Carne Details

PMF Score: 83

Design: 25 out of 30
Challenge: 23 out of 30
Condition: 17 out of 20
19th Hole: 18 out of 20
Price: €55 on weekdays and weekends. (About half-price Nov. to Feb.) You can also get a discount if you play before 8 am.
Length: Blue: 6,730 yards
White: 6,400 yards
Buggies and Trolleys: Both, and caddies too.

Tee Times: No restricted days for visitors. 25% deposit required. 100% refund as long as you give at least 28-days notice.

Carne Golf Links

Belmullet
Co. Mayo, Ireland
Tel. (353-97) 82292
Fax. 81477
e-mail: carngolf@iol.ie
www.carnegolflinks.com

Donegal Golf Club

Founded in 1976
Donegal, Co. Donegal

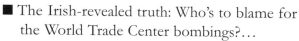

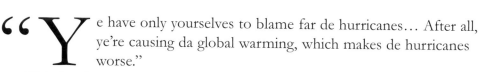

PMF
79
Score

- The Irish-revealed truth: Who's to blame for the World Trade Center bombings?…
- The best spot in Ireland for a thatched-roof vacation cottage…
- Pat Ruddy's only disappointment… and more

" **Y**e have only yourselves to blame far de hurricanes… After all, ye're causing da global warming, which makes de hurricanes worse."

This is what an Irish construction worker told me in a bar in Donegal. We also learned on this trip that:

1) The CIA was actually the group responsible for sending planes into the World Trade Centers on 9/11, and...

2) Most American women are now getting premature C-sections, so that they don't gain too much weight during pregnancy.

It's funny how stereotypes work—they always seem accurate until they are about you.

The Irish, like most people, are willing to believe almost anything they read in the newspaper. And during my most recent trip, what really sold newspapers in Ireland was anti-American stories.

In addition to arguments with the locals, we were in Donegal to play a very long golf course, called Donegal Golf Club. Locals call it Murvagh, the name of the nearby town.

First, let me set the record straight: I love Donegal. The Northwest is my favorite part of the country. My wife's

In the 1600s, some people believed the entrance to Purgatory was found in Donegal. It's not hard to understand why.

family roots are in Letterkenny. And when I eventually have the opportunity to spend a month or two every year living in Ireland, one of my top choices will be the Northwest.

Donegal is a nice links course—it's in the top 25, but not one of the country's best. The November 2004 issue of *Golf World Magazine* ranked Donegal as one of the top 10 golf courses in Ireland. These folks obviously have not played every links course in the country. (Keep in mind: This is a third-tier links course, but it's still better than almost anything you can play in the United States. That's how good links golf is.)

Donegal's main challenge is that it's long—really long. Nearly 7,400 yards from the tips and nearly 7,000 yards from the white tees.

The fairways here, however, are fairly wide and forgiving. The main problem I have with the place is that you never get to play along the coast, or among the high dunes. In fact, you rarely get to even see the water. Instead, you play inland behind the big dunes. That's a shame, because the dunes are fantastic.

This is one of Pat Ruddy's redesigns. Easily his weakest effort. I wonder if the folks in charge gave Mr. Ruddy enough leeway.

We played Donegal on a day that is typically Irish, but unheard of almost anywhere else in the world. It rained like hell for the entire front nine. The winds and the chill made it especially miserable. Then on the back

My main problem with Donegal is that you don't get to play along the coast.

12ᴛʜTEE

nine it cleared up completely... sunny skies and barely a whisper of breeze. The lesson: Never leave your rain gear in the car, no matter how clear the skies look when you start.

Donegal is one of my favorite parts of Ireland. If I was looking to rent a cottage in the summer, this is one of the places I'd look.

■ **What's good:** A long links course, 7,000 yards from the white tees and 6,500 from the green (what the Irish call the "society" tees). Donegal is more wide open than tight links tracts such as Enniscrone, Ballybunion, or Lahinch. The main challenge here is the length. This is a very enjoyable round of golf. You get the full experience without the extreme accuracy required at the top links courses. Rough is a lot more forgiving. The nicest on-the-course toilets I've ever seen... great clubhouse and bar and outdoor area that overlook the 18th hole.

■ **What's not:** Mostly flat with only a few ocean views because a huge string of dunes runs along the coastline.

■ **Best hole:** Par-5, 550-yard 8th hole. This is a great hole. It has twists and turns, elevation changes, dunes and hollows, everything you want in a great links challenge. It can be a par-6 or -7 if you're playing into the wind.

Donegal Details

PMF Score: 79
Design: 21 out of 30
Challenge: 24 out of 30
Condition: 17 out of 20
19th hole: 17 out of 20
Price: €55 Monday to Thursday
€70 Fri-Sun and holidays
Length: Blue: 7,381 yards
White: 6,921 yards
Buggies and Trolleys: Both
Tee Times: Any day. Sundays

restricted to 11am to 1pm. 25% deposit required. Cancel more than 21 days, full refund. After that, no refund.

Donegal Golf Club
Murvagh, Laghey
Co. Donegal, Ireland
Tel. (353-74) 973-4054
Fax. 973-4377
e-mail: info@donegalgolfclub.ie
www.donegalgolfclub.ie

Dunfanaghy Golf Club

Founded in 1906
Dunfanaghy, Co. Donegal

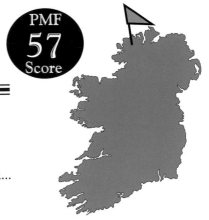

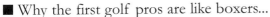

■ Why the first golf pros are like boxers...
■ Greatest golfer of the first 100 years...
■ The man who introduced golf to America...
  and more

T here's not much to say about Dunfanaghy Golf Club. It's not a very good course. But the story behind the man who designed it is a lot more interesting. This man was the greatest golfer of the sport's first 100 years. And although most Americans have never heard of him, he is as responsible as anyone for making the game popular in the United States. Let me give you the full details...

Golf pros simply don't know how good they have it today. You see, for the sport's first five or six decades, the most respected men in the game were amateurs, not professionals.

The best amateurs came from wealthy families, or had made enough money on their own to have the time to pursue golf as a serious hobby. Golf as a profession, however, was frowned upon as "ungentlemanly," even "uncivilized."

As a result, the first generation of professional golf pros—including the greatest golfer of the sport's first 100 years—came from the poorest families. As Mark Frost says in his fantastic book, *The Greatest Game Ever Played*, "Not unlike boxers, the first wave of golf pros used the sport to elevate themselves from gnawing poverty."

Even for those who made it, success was a solid middle-class lifestyle, not the riches pro golfers reap today. No private transportation. No agents. No first-class hotels. No lucrative endorsement contracts. As Frost reports:

> "Professionals who harbored any hope of advancement in
> the game lived an itinerant existence, traveling by third-
> class rail and hitching rides on farm wagons to remote

tournament sites, bunking in cheap rooming houses, eating common meals, and closing the local pubs. They occupied a lowly rung on the social ladder... "

Professionals and amateurs competed in tournaments together, including the British Open. Amateurs received a warm welcome, and often became honorary members of the hosting club. Professionals, meanwhile, were expected to keep out of sight. It wasn't until the 1920s that pros were allowed to eat lunch or even change clothes in a private clubhouse in the U.S. or Britain. In Ireland, when Eddie Hackett became the head golf pro of Portmarnock in 1939, he was told to move his car from the parking lot and to eat his lunch in the kitchen, not the dining room.

Frost's *Greatest Game* is the story of golf's greatest hardscrabble early pro: Harry Vardon.

Born on the island of Jersey, about 80 miles south of the British mainland, Harry and his family were dirt poor. At the age of 14, Harry was signed into a position of three-year servitude for a local doctor. His menial wages went straight to his mother and alcoholic father.

At 17 Vardon got a job as a gardener for the captain of the local Jersey golf club. When the man saw the young boy's swing, he immediately took the boy on as his playing partner. The two dominated local club matches, and Vardon was soon the best player on the island. Vardon left Jersey at 20 and spent the next few years with his brother in northern England, eking out a living as a golf pro. He made the equivalent of about $90 a week in today's money.

But Vardon worked hard on his game and was soon the greatest golfer in the world. In 1900 he went on a barnstorming trip around the United States. It is probably the most significant event in U.S. golf history because it introduced the entire country to the game.

The sport became so popular so quickly that U.S. golfers took up the sport in record numbers, and would soon dominate the game all over the world—a position they have held for nearly 100 years.

Harry's tour around America pitted him against the top two or three golfers at the country's top clubs, who played their better score against Harry's.

On the 88-match tour, Harry broke the scoring record on half the courses he visited. He lost just once (match play, 2 and 1) to a local pro in Miami.

Americans had never seen a sporting performance anything like it.

When Harry played an exhibition match at America's first public golf course (Van Cortland Park in New York), the stock exchange shut down so traders could watch the match in the Bronx.

Despite contracting tuberculosis, which left him with a trembling hand that often made short putts impossible, Vardon won six British Opens—more than any other man in history. The number would certainly have been even higher, but after his 1914 win, the championship was cancelled for five straight years because of World War I.

Late in his career, Harry threw himself into a life of teaching and course design. One of Harry's courses is a short links track in northwest Ireland called Dunfanaghy.

Frost's *The Greatest Game Ever Played* is easily the best golf book I've ever read. You'll be amazed at how the game has changed over the past 100 years.

Off to Donegal When You're Dead

In the Catholic religion, you go to purgatory when you die.

Unless you lived a saintly life—then you go straight to Heaven. Or if you were really bad—then you go straight to hell. But most ordinary people who are only occasionally bad must first spend time in purgatory to pay for their sins.

The good news is that everyone who goes to purgatory eventually gets to go to Heaven. The bad news is that one moment of pain and suffering in purgatory is worse than anything suffered on Earth. Even worse, the torments of your soul in purgatory could take thousands of years… before you get to move on to a better place.

When Shakespeare was alive in the early 1600s, many Catholics (British and Irish) believed that there was an entrance to purgatory through a cave in Donegal—which was discovered by St. Patrick.

You can see why they believed Donegal had other-worldly significance. The scenery is just spectacular: giant cliffs, crashing Atlantic waves, mountains, rivers, streams and lakes, and whipping winds and rain like you've never seen before.

Unfortunately, as I mentioned in the beginning of this chapter, Harry Vardon's 1905 Dunfanaghy layout falls short of his spectacular golf game.

Situated on the shores of Sheephaven Bay, and right next to the Derryveagh Mountains, the course offers magnificent views, but little else.

Dunfanaghy has a few spectacular holes, but the rest of the course is hardly worth playing unless you are staying right next door. Even then, I'd recommend making the short drive to the two spectacular links at nearby Rosapenna.

One interesting feature of Dunfanaghy are the many burns (creeks) that meander through the fairways, reminiscent of St. Andrews.

And as I mentioned, there is a great stretch of spectacular holes: #s8–10, which are much better than the rest of the course. Number nine is a par-3 over a beach… and #10 is a big dogleg right that tempts you to take a short cut over the beach. Number 17 is a great par-3 as well. In fact, #9 and #17 are as good as any par-3s in the region. But, unfortunately, four holes does not a golf course make.

This course needs a makeover in a big way.

- **What's good:** The history—designed by the greatest golfer of the game's first 100 years. You can hit it anywhere off the tee and still have a shot at the green… the burns make the course harder than it looks… it will make you feel good about your golf game after playing tough Irish links… good for the really high handicapper… the course looks great compared to the €5 pitch-and-putt course adjacent to it. Paul McGinley, one of Ireland's top PGA pros, grew up and began playing golf here.

- **What's not:** Not interesting or challenging enough to be worth your time, unless you are staying nearby for a long time, and can't make it to Rosapenna. Course is played inland, for the most part, away from the dunes that guard the coast.

- **Best hole:** Par-4 #10. You can cut the corner from the tee with a big drive that carries the beach. This is a great hole—a few more like it and Dunfanaghy would be a course worth playing.

Dunfanaghy Details

PMF Score: 57
Design: 14 out of 30
Challenge: 14 out of 30
Condition: 14 out of 20
19th hole: 15 out of 20
Price: €30 on weekdays
€35 on weekends
Length: 5,474 yards
Buggies and Trolleys: Both

Tee Times: No restrictions or deposits, but weekends are busy.

Dunfanaghy Golf Club
Dunfanaghy, Letterkenny
Co. Donegal
Tel. (353-74) 91 36335
Fax. 36684
dunfanaghygolf@eircom.net
www.dunfanaghygolfclub.com

Enniscrone Golf Club

PMF
88
Score

Founded in 1918
Enniscrone, Co. Sligo

- The man who saved Irish golf in the twentieth century...
- Where to hide dead Viking invaders...
- One of Ireland's most underrated links... and more

Want to know what golf was like in Ireland before the days of 6-month-in-advance tee-time deposits, foursomes who arrive by helicopter, and €250 rounds?

Then read about Eddie Hackett, the country's most famous and prolific golf course designer.

You'd probably never heard of Eddie Hackett before you picked up this book. Few Americans have. But he's one of the most important men in Irish golf of the past 100 years.

Hackett was born in a Dublin pub (no kidding) in 1910. He had a hard childhood. His family, like most Irish at the time, was extremely poor. Hackett was hospitalized for long stretches with tuberculosis, but he picked up the game of golf after his father became one of the first working class Catholics to get into an Irish golf club.

Hackett learned how to make golf clubs at the Royal Dublin Golf Club, and later became the pro at Portmarnock—although he was never allowed in the clubhouse and was paid only I£10 a week.

Keep in mind, at the time pros weren't treated much better in the United States. A job as a golf pro in the first part of the twentieth century was not the cushy job it is today. Back then pros had to bust their butts and hustle for every penny they earned. And they got virtually no respect... even from the places that employed them. At the U.S. Open in the early part of the century, amateurs changed in the luxurious clubhouse locker room. Pros were not allowed inside. (See the Dunfanaghy chapter for more details.)

In the 1950s, Hackett left golf and proved to be much worse at business than the game he loved. He came back to golf in the 1960s, when the Golfing

Union of Ireland asked him to give clinics around the country. Hackett then fumbled his way through the design of one of Ireland's first full-size golf courses in nearly three decades. All of a sudden, he was an architect—basically the only one in all of Ireland. Remember, even in the 1960s, golf was only a game

Many courses have shelters such as this one at Enniscrone, where you can get out of the wind and rain.

for the wealthy. Very few new courses were being built in these lean years.

But if there *was* a golf course to be built in Ireland between 1960 and 1990, Eddie Hackett was the man for the job. Mostly because he was really cheap.

Hackett designed his courses simply by walking the land. No fancy computers. No aerial photos, models, or drawings. No blueprints. Hackett charged just a few hundred pounds for his work, and very often received nothing at all. When he worked on the course at Connemara, for example, he told the club to pay him whenever they could.

Hackett's basic strategy was to move as little earth as possible. As he told the authors of the excellent book, *Links of Heaven:* "I could never break up the earth the way they tell me Jack [Nicklaus] and Arnold [Palmer] do. You disrupt the soil profile and anyway, it's unnatural. I use what's there within reason. You're only as good as what the Lord gives you in features. And you can never do with trees what you can do with sand dunes."

Hackett worked on a slew of courses on Ireland's west coast—some of which are among the top links in the country: Waterville, Dingle, Connemara, Rosapenna (Old), Carne, Donegal, and one of the best links courses in Ireland you've probably never heard of: Enniscrone.

Enniscrone is a classic links course that ranks up with the country's very best (in my top 12). The course gets very little mention, but it's worth going well out of your way to play. You'll often see Enniscrone and Carne listed together as "undiscovered" gems in the Northwest, but to me Enniscrone is a much better course right now.

It is in fantastic condition, and has everything going for it that a great links course should have: high dunes, blind shots, elevation changes, fantastic greens, high grass, and dramatic views. And it's also one of the best links bargains in the world.

On the main course, holes 3-5 and 14-16 are Donald Steel's redesigns. All the rest are Eddie Hackett originals.

Look out for the giant dune on the 14th fairway known in Gaelic as *Cnoc na gCorp* (the hill of the bodies). It reputedly contains the corpses of vanquished Viking invaders.

■ **What's good:** True, long links test, lots and lots of high grass surrounding fairways and greens. It's long—6,800 yards from the whites. Probably too hard for the average golfer. Move up to the green tees if necessary. Located close to towns and other courses… affordable rates—about half the price of many other top-20 courses… lots of trouble if you miss the fairways and greens.

Rumor has it that the dunes of Enniscrone's 14th fairway are the burial grounds of Viking invaders.

Better than Carne, which gets more attention.

- **What's not:** Not many bunkers… too hard for the golfer who doesn't strike the ball well and hit it accurately most of the time.
- **Best hole:** #16, a snaking, dogleg-right par-5 between high dunes, with a green that starts to turn back to the left.

Enniscrone Details

PMF Score: 88
Design: 26 out of 30
Challenge: 27 out of 30
Condition: 18 out of 20
19th hole: 17 out of 20
Price: €50 on weekdays
€65 on weekends
Length: Blue: 6,948 yards
White: 6,814; Green: 6,372
Buggies and Trolleys: Both

Tee Times: Any day. Phone for tee time. No deposit required.

Enniscrone Golf Club
Enniscrone
Co. Sligo, Ireland
Tel. (353-96) 36297
Fax. 36657
e-mail: enniscronegolf@eircom.net
www.enniscronegolf.com

Narin & Portnoo Golf Club

Founded in 1930
Portnoo, Co. Donegal

- How to play links golf as it existed 50 years ago…
- Take a free drop from behind the cows…
- Where undiscovered Ireland still exists…
  and more

I t's amazing the changes that have taken place in Ireland in just the past 10 years. When I first visited in 1995 to visit my girlfriend (now wife), Ireland was one of the cheapest places in all of Europe.

There wasn't a single golf course in the country that cost more than $100 per round. Irish links were probably the greatest golf bargain in the world back then.

But today Ireland is one of the most expensive places in Europe. Dublin is every bit as expensive as London and Paris. Most of Ireland's golf courses are no longer the bargains they once were.

But great bargains do still exist. You just have to look a little harder now, as I did on my recent trip. One of the great bargains is a completely undiscovered place called Narin & Portnoo, located on a small peninsula northwest of Donegal town.

Narin & Portnoo is a place where the game exists as it did 50 or 60 years ago. There are no modern conveniences. The club owns only four golf carts. There's no pro shop. The clubhouse looks like no one has given it a coat of paint in 20 years. The carpet looks older than me. But

Narin & Portnoo has recently undergone a major renovation, which added almost 1,000 yards.

the golf… well… it's quite spectacular at times.

We played Narin & Portnoo on a sunny but breezy Monday morning in early October. The place was deserted.

We pulled into the parking lot at 9:30 am, and waited 30 minutes for someone to show up in the pro shop. When no one did, we put money into the self-serve trolley machine and began our round.

Over the next three hours we saw more cows than golfers. In fact, sometimes the course is referred to as "Port-moo" because the local cows at one time roamed the fairways. They were all behind fences on our visit.

Narin & Portnoo has the type of land that could make for a spectacular links course—the dunes and cliffs and seaside holes are amazing. And Narin & Portnoo is, right now, probably the most unpretentious links course in the country.

When I played the course, there were a few things that landed Portnoo in the third tier of courses. (That could change very soon, as I'll explain in a minute.)

For one, the first four holes are uninteresting and uninspiring. You could be playing any flat parkland course in the world.

Things begin to pick up in a big way on #5. And the rest of the holes are startlingly good. Number 8 is a great par-3 over a huge cavernous expanse of high grass. It would be considered a great hole on even the best courses. Nine is a tremendous downhill 300-yard hole that tempts you to drive the green, especially with the wind behind you. Ten is a great uphill tee shot, with a steep cliff to the right. Slice it and your ball will find the

This is spectacular terrain, one of the country's undiscovered gems. It's cheap, too: just €30 on weekdays.

bottom of the Atlantic. The tee box is surrounded on three sides by rocks and water.

The other major problem with Narin & Portnoo when I played it, was the length. It was ridiculously short—just 5,935 yards... and par of 69.

The good news is that the course is undergoing a major renovation, and should be complete as I write. It will add almost 1,000 yards to the overall layout.

The plans were posted in the clubhouse during my visit in late 2004, and most of the construction took place in 2005. As I was putting this chapter together, Tom Plunkett, the pro at Narin & Portnoo, told me the new course will officially open in the spring of 2006. Par will now be 72 instead of 69. The course will now be more than 6,700 yards. There are seven brand-new greens and lots of new bunkers.

Only in Ireland: The best golfer Narin & Portnoo has ever produced is a reverand.

If this redesign is done well, Portnoo could easily move up 10 spots or more—the natural terrain is that good.

Here's something you'll find only in Ireland: The best golfer the club has ever produced is a man named Brendan McBride. What's unusual about McBride is that he's a priest, who is now the Irish chaplain in San Francisco. Father McBride once held the amateur course record at Narin & Portnoo (64) and also broke the course record at Donegal in 1975 when he shot a 68.

■ **What's good:** Great value, only €35 on weekends... this is a real links course... very hilly... dramatic views... course is probably empty all the time... big cliffs and sharp doglegs... fairly wide open, which is nice for higher handicappers. About as unpretentious as a golf course can be... cows come right up to the course on the adjacent farmland. Harry Vardon is said to have helped with the early design while vacationing here in the early 1900s. No reservation fees required for tee times. No cancellations fees either. Redesign should move this course up in the rankings considerably.

■ **What's not:** It's not upscale by any means... golf course living here means mobile homes, some of which are situated between the course and the sea.

■ **Best hole:** #9 is a dramatic 325-yard downhill par-4 that will tempt you to bring out your driver- er, especially if the wind is

Number 9, shown here, is reachable off the tee, just 325 yards downhill and often downwind. Just don't miss left or right.

behind you. You can easily make 3... or triple bogey if you can't keep the ball out of the Atlantic.

Narin & Portnoo Details

PMF Score: 77
Design: 24 out of 30
Challenge: 22 out of 30
Condition: 16 out of 20
19th hole: 15 out of 20
Price: €30 on weekdays
    €35 on weekends
Length: New design will be
    6,700 yards.
Buggies and Trolleys: Both (but there are only four buggies for the entire course).

Tee Times: Any day is okay except early Sunday morning (before noon). No deposit required.

Narin & Portnoo Golf Club
Narin, Portnoo
Co. Donegal, Ireland
Tel. (353-74) 954-5107
Fax. 954-5994
e-mail: narinportnoo@eircom.net
www.narinportnoogolfclub.ie

North West Golf Club

PMF
61
Score

Founded in 1891
Buncrana, Co. Donegal

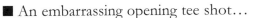

- An embarrassing opening tee shot…
- A disappearing golf course…
- Where to find the warmest welcome in Ireland…
  and more

"Junior" was nervous when he stepped to the tee. More nervous than he'd been on any tee shot in his life. And with good reason.

You see, Junior had just been elected "Captain" of North West Golf Club. Traditionally, the captain hits the first drive of the spring season. This is a big event that takes place at every golf club in Ireland.

So Junior took a deep breath. He tried to stay calm. He placed his tee in the ground, smiled at the few dozen onlookers and photographers from the local paper, and went through his customary pre-shot routine.

A few waggles, another deep breath… and a quick glance down the first fairway.

Then he took the club back and, feeling good, took a good rip to open the new golf season at one of the oldest clubs in the country.

Thirty yards ahead, a photographer crouched in preparation for the shot… well off to one side.

"You might want to stand back a bit," members had told him earlier. "No worries," said the photographer, eager to get a good shot.

He never had a chance.

Junior snap-hooked his drive left. It hit the photographer in the elbow and broke the bone in two.

The photographer did, however, get a great shot. On the clubhouse wall you'll find the photo of the ball in mid-flight. Look at the gasps on faces in the crowd. They can see the ball about to hit the photographer.

North West Golf Club is located on the Loch Swilly, just south of the town of Buncrana.

The welcome we got at North West Golf Club was unbelievable. It was, without a doubt, the friendliest place we went on our entire one-month journey.

I only wish I could report better things about the golf course.

The club has an amazing history—it's been around since 1891 and is one of the only clubs in the country that has wel-comed Catholics and Protestants in equal

During "The Troubles," political murals covered walls in the North. But Protestants and Catholics still played golf together at North West GC.

numbers for most of its existence. As the members told me: "There were never any signs of 'The Troubles' here."

We played North West with two long-time members, Dudley and Sean. First, they beat us in a four-ball match. Then they gave us drinks, sandwich-es, and even necktie souvenirs. We had to leave before they could invite us over for dinner.

It's a shame the golf at North West is not as nice as the people who play there.

North West is a short course of only 6,335 yards from the back tees. Unfortunately, the place has lost enormous amounts of land due to erosion. The guys I played with told me the pro used to have to hit an 8-iron from the pro shop to reach the adjacent lake. Now he can do it with an easy pitching wedge.

This means the layout has changed dramatically over the years. Many fairways are now right on top of each other. Several, in fact, cross one another. Fairways #4 and #17 cross, so do 17 and 18. Then there's #16… which is the one of the shortest holes I've ever seen: just 93 yards from the back tees.

Still, despite the fact that the golf is mediocre at best, it's a place worth visiting if you want to have an enjoyable day. You'll likely meet some very friendly folks, and you'll get to play one of the oldest courses in Ireland.

■ **What's good:** Warm welcome… a place where Northern and Republic folks have played golf together for decades, even through "The Troubles." Scenic views of Loch Swilly… nice view from clubhouse… easy to get a tee time… cheap.

■ **What's not:** Course is nothing to get excited about. It's played on about a 200-yard-wide stretch of land between a road and a loch, a giant mountain looms over the course behind the main road. Holes are often right on top of one another, and some even cross fairways. We played from the green tees because it was a "society day." You should definitely play from the tips. It's short, easy, and pretty wide open except for a few holes that run along the road.

■ **Best hole:** #10… a tough 400-yard par-4 with out-of-bounds up the whole right side, and a burn to cross before the green.

North West Details

PMF Score: 61
Design: 15 out of 30
Challenge: 13 out of 30
Condition: 15 out of 20
19th hole: 18 out of 20
Price: €20 on weekdays
    €25 on weekends
Length: White: 6,335 yards
    Yellow: 6,171 yards
Buggies and Trolleys: Trolleys only

and no caddies.
Tee Times: No restrictions, but weekends are crowded.

North West Golf Club
Lisfannon, Fahan
Buncrana, Co. Donegal, Ireland
Tel. (353-74) 936-1715
Fax. 936-3284
e-mail: nwgc@tinet.ie
website: None

Portsalon Golf Club

Founded in 1891
Fanad, Co. Donegal

PMF
92
Score

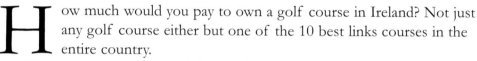

- One of the best links courses in Ireland;
  price: $80,000...
- The best links bargain in Ireland—just $40
  (weekends included)
- The course the experts forgot... and more

H ow much would you pay to own a golf course in Ireland? Not just
any golf course either but one of the 10 best links courses in the
entire country.

Would you pay a million dollars... $5 million... more?

Well, what if I told you this place is not only a top-10 course, but is also
full of history and charm (founded in 1891) and is located on one of the
most beautiful beaches in the nation.

Enough suspense. The course I'm talking about is Portsalon Golf Club.
And although it's hard to believe, it was for sale not too long ago for an
incredibly cheap $80,000.

It was 1984 to be exact. That shows you just how far the country has
come in the past 20 years.

Portsalon is located directly on Ballymacstocker Bay, and 110 years ago
was one of the best golf courses in the world. An article in the British magazine *Golfing* said it was "one of the best, if not the best course in Ireland."

Like most of the other courses in Ireland at the time, it was a place
for British aristocracy. Colonel B.J. Barton founded the place, which
included a grand hotel and a steamer ferry to carry guests to the train station south of the resort.

The local Irish were dirt-poor—they carried golf clubs and worked at
the hotel. But the local British were rich, and Portsalon did well until World
War II. Then things fell apart.

There were very few visitors for the next 40 years. The 1975 course
records show £175 in paid green fees, collected at a local bar.

A few years later the hotel caught fire and the land, including the golf
course, was put up for sale in 1984. The price: an incredible I£68,000—the

equivalent of about $80,000 according to the exchange rate at the time.

Locals sold lottery tickets and bought the course.

They took over in 1986. But the course was not in very good shape. Golf writer Tom Doak visited soon after, and described the place in his book, *The Confidential Guide to Golf Courses*:

Portsalon is easily the best links bargain in all of Ireland. It costs just €35 on weekdays, and about $500 for an entire season.

> "I hardly know what to report. I'm not even sure [the course] was still there when I saw it. The first few holes seemed to be still in use, though the fairways consisted mainly of clover, and a white ball would have been impossible to locate, and the holes themselves were marked with only the shortest pieces of plastic pipe and a makeshift flag. I can't recommend a course which I'm not even sure is still there, but it was indeed a lovely, quiet spot, and I enjoyed the puzzle it presented immensely."

Mr. Doak gave Portsalon a 3 on a 10-point scale. My how things have changed.

Portsalon has undergone a major transformation. After redesign work in 2001-2002 by Pat Ruddy (Ireland's best local designer, and owner of The European Club), the folks at Portsalon now have one of the 10 best links courses in all of Ireland. And the country's best-kept golf secret.

Without a doubt, Portsalon was the best discovery of my entire trip.

I hadn't heard anything about the place. Didn't have any expectations. The tiny parking lot and shabby clubhouse led me to believe it was a mediocre course at best. The expectations didn't get any higher when I saw the greens fees posted on the clubhouse wall: €35 on weekdays and €40 on weekends.

But after a bit of a letdown of a first hole… wow… the place is just stunning.

Portsalon has everything a great links course should have: elevated tees… high dunes… views of the beach and water… and interesting twists and turns through low-lying valleys.

I've never seen anyone put this course anywhere near Ireland's top 10, but that's probably because few "experts" have actually played the place.

If you get anywhere near this course, make sure you visit. I promise you won't be disappointed. And get this: For just €400 (about $500), you can become a year-long member. You don't have to pay another penny to play the rest of the year.

In other words, you can play Portsalon for an entire year for about what it costs to play Old Head or Doonbeg once.

Keep in mind: This is still a completely undiscovered place—but that probably won't last long. In fact, it's such a good discovery, I hesitate to even mention it here. I hate the idea that some day Portsalon will be overrun with American visitors. But greens fees could double and it will still be a bargain.

■ **What's good:** The best golf value in all of Ireland (just €35 on weekdays)… great history—it was one of the founding courses in the Golfing Union of Ireland… one of the best designs in the country… huge variety of holes: some with very wide fairways and elevated tees, others with very tight valley-like typical links holes… great views of a beautiful beach and the Knockalla Mountains all around… long, tough, and challenging course… friendly welcome… no crazy tee-time policies or cancellation penalties… completely unpretentious members and friendly welcome in the club-house… giant double greens like those at St. Andrews.

■ **What's not:** It's a fairly flat course compared to some others in the top 10… no pro shop to speak of… and

The Knockalla Mountains offer a great backdrop to one side of Portsalon… the beach and sea to the other.

the restaurant and bar could certainly use an upgrade. No website, but there is an e-mail address.

■ Best hole:

Number 2 is a great 435-yard par-4. It's also a dogleg left over the river, from an elevated tee. The second shot is a tough one if you don't hit a great drive. You might even have to lay up, especially on a windy day.

It's hard to believe you could have bought one of the top-10 links courses in Ireland for just $80,000—that's what Portsalon sold for in 1984.

Portsalon Details

PMF Score: 92

Design: 28 out of 30
Challenge: 29 out of 30
Condition: 18 out of 20
19th hole: 17 out of 20
Price: €35 on weekdays
€40 Fri. - Sunday
Length: White: 6,810 yards
Yellow: 6,570 yards
Green: 6,043 yards

Buggies and Trolleys: Both
Tee Times: Call for time—no restrictions or deposits needed. A simple call is all that's required.

Portsalon Golf Club

Fanad, Co. Donegal, Ireland
Tel. (353-74) 915-9459
Fax. 915-9919
portsalongolfclub@eircom.net
website: none

Rosapenna Golf Club

**Sandy Hills Links and
Morris-Ruddy Links
Founded in 1893
Rosapenna, Co. Donegal**

■ The best links resort in Ireland...
■ Four famous designers on one course...
■ Nine new holes from Pat Ruddy... and more

I n 1962, a fire broke out in the crowded guest wing of the Rosapenna Hotel. Most people stuffed their belongings into their suitcases as quickly as possible, and scurried from the smokey building. But one guest, The Duke of St. Albans, ordered another bowl of soup. It's reported he wanted to be the last man to eat at "Old Rosapenna." Richard Phinney recounts the story in his book, *Links of Heaven.*

The fire brought an end to what was, in the early part of the twentieth century, one of the most luxurious hotels in the country, complete with its own orchestra, a wine cellar, and a ballroom for black-tie affairs. Besides a fine links golf course, there was croquet, lawn tennis, hunting, fishing, and horseback riding for the wealthy guests.

After the fire, a less-glamorous hotel was built, which saw years of deterioration and neglect.

Then, in 1981, Frank Casey, the son of the man who served the Duke of St. Albans his last bowl of soup, bought the hotel and golf complex for I£500,000. Casey still runs the place today, and now has, without

We took a Land Rover tour with head greenskeeper, Jack Green, who built the new Rosapenna course with Pat Ruddy.

a doubt, the best links golf resort in the country.

The hotel is first rate, with large rooms and spectacular views of both the courses and the sea. There's a nice swimming pool, and a very good hotel restaurant. (The rundown tennis court is my only complaint, but I can't imagine it's ever calm enough here for tennis.) And the golf is, well... fantastic.

Rosapenna has two links courses. The first, until this year, was called the Old Tom Morris Course. It was built and redesigned by some of the most famous men of early twentieth-century golf—Harry Vardon, Tom Morris, James Braid, and H.S. Colt. I played the old version of this course—it was a decent introduction to links golf.

Now, however, they've completely scrapped the back nine (which was much weaker than the front), and have added nine new holes designed by the great Pat Ruddy. The course is now called the Morris-Ruddy links. This course just opened in June 2005. They've added 900 yards. It's now 7,100 yards from the tips.

The other golf course at Rosapenna is called Sandy Hills—and it is simply amazing. This is the course to play if you have time for only one round at Rosapenna.

It was designed by (guess who?) Pat Ruddy—who's done most of the best links design work in Ireland in the last few years. The course first

I haven't seen the new Morris-Ruddy back nine, but if it's anything like Sandy Hills, it will be a great course.

opened for play in 2003.

Working with Pat Ruddy was the head greenskeeper, the appropriately named Jack Green. The two decided on the layout by simply walking the land. They didn't use architectural drawings or schematics. They simply walked the turf and roughed out sketches. They started with hole #1 and kept going till they had finished #18.

Sandy Hills is one of the 10-best courses in Ireland. It has everything you want in a great links experience—tremendous dunes, deep valleys, elevated tees, tricky bunkers, closely guarded greens. This is a tough course, especially if you play it on a really windy day, as we did. If you can't hit it low and straight, you'll be stuck with more penalty strokes than you've ever had before.

In short, the Rosapenna complex is a great golf getaway, especially if you want to spend several days in one spot, without having to re-pack your bags every day.

Keep in mind that Portsalon (another top-10 links) is only 30 minutes away, which means you can stay in a great hotel (Rosapenna), enjoy great meals (also at Rosapenna), and play two of Ireland's top-10 courses, without

Rosapenna is the top two-course links resort in Ireland right now. Two great courses and a very nice hotel.

The front nine of the Morris-Ruddy Links, which plays out on fairly flat land near the coast.

ever having to pack up your suitcase. That's a rarity in Ireland, because most of the great links courses are very spread out. The only other place in the country with two top courses this close together is the Northern Ireland coast, where you'll find Portstewart and Portrush. Another bonus: Right next to Rosapenna, St. Patrick's two courses are being redesigned by Jack Nicklaus. Soon there will be four great links courses in a five-mile radius.

And at Rosapenna, you can come back to the hotel and enjoy the snooker table, the pool, whirlpool, steam room, and spa, before having drinks in the bar and a great dinner overlooking the bay.

What's great is that the place is really affordable. Even at the most expensive times, a room costs only €95 a night, and you can get package deals and off-season rates to save considerably.

Sandy Hills Golf Links

■ **What's good:** This is a great golf course—when it has some time to mature, it could move up even higher on Ireland's top-10 list. Spectacular links design with everything going for it. Good value… you can probably get a time whenever you want to play. Frank Casey and his staff provide great service. Frank is around the hotel to run the business by day, then dons black tie apparel to welcome guests to dinner in the elegant dining room in the evening.

■ **What's not:** There are a few places where the turf is worn or diseased but

111

remember, this course was only two years old when I played it. Frank Green is the head groundskeeper and is fanatical about keeping this course in top shape. From the white tees it's a very tough course if you don't hit the ball consistently long and straight. There are many doglegs, and you've got to be accurate or you'll never find your tee shots. This is one course where you might want to move up a set of tees—there are three sets for men: blue, white, and yellow. From the blues, this is one of the most challenging links in the country at over 7,000 yards.

■ **Best hole:** So many good holes, but my favorite is #10, a 405-yard par-4 with tremendous dunes on each side, and the Muckish Mountains in the background beyond the green.

Old Tom Morris Links

Remember, I played the Old Tom Morris course, not the new Morris-Ruddy Links. Numbers 1-9 are the same, but Pat Ruddy's back nine is brand new. So my comments here are only about the original front nine.

■ **What's good:** If you get beat up on the Sandy Hills Links, you'll feel much better about your game after playing the Tom Morris course. Great history here—designed by some of the most famous names in golf. Two holes (no longer in use) crossed the road—not an auxiliary road, but a real road, where

Rosapenna's Sandy Hills Links is a bargain in the off-season... just €50.

cars drive 40-50 miles per hour. For the most part, this links is wide open—you can miss the fairway and still have a decent approach. Short enough for high handicappers to play.

■ **What's not:** Shrubbery blocks your views of the sea. It's played on basically flat and uninteresting land (especially compared to Sandy Hills), with only a few elevation changes. Short for championship course and much easier than the Sandy Hills links.

■ **Best hole:** The two holes that cross the road, #s 11 and 18, were the most exciting. Your playing partner had to watch for cars and let you know when it was safe to play. These holes are now gone.

Rosapenna Details

Sandy Hills Golf Links
PMF Score: 92

Design: 28 out of 30
Challenge: 29 out of 30
Condition: 17 out of 20
19th hole: 18 out of 20
Price: €75 in high season
    €50 in off season
Length: Blue: 7,155 yards; White: 6,356; Yellow: 5,787
Buggies and Trolleys: Both
Tee Times: Any day. No restrictions or deposit required for a tee time.

Morris-Ruddy Links
PMF Score: 73

Design: 20 out of 30
Challenge: 18 out of 30
Condition: 17 out of 20
19th hole: 18 out of 20
Price: €50 in high season
    €40 in off season
Length: From the tips, new course is 7,100 yards.
Buggies and Trolleys: Both
Tee Times: Same as Sandy Hills

Rosapenna Hotel and Golf Links

Downings
Co. Donegal, Ireland
Tel. (353-74) 915-5301
Fax. 915-5128
e-mail: rosapenna@eircom.net
www.rosapenna.ie

Co. Sligo Golf Club

Founded in 1894
Rosses Point, Co. Sligo

- A social club you want to avoid on the links...
- Ireland's best poet—and the world's best poem...
- Add five stokes for your back-nine score...
  and more

When you play golf in Ireland, you forget what it's like to play the typical agonizing weekend round on a public golf course in America.

You see, the Irish play fast. Really fast. As my buddy Murphy said, "Golf is the only thing the Irish do fast."

Here, it's hard to play a round that takes longer than four hours. When you first start playing golf in Ireland, you'll feel like you have to practically run just to keep up.

We were cruising through our trip covering 44 courses in 30 days. We were able to squeeze many rounds in as little as three and a half hours.

Then... we got to County Sligo's Rosses Point.

We played on a society-outing day. Ireland is full of "societies," which are basically social clubs that often organize golf outings and take over an entire course.

In addition to the society outing, the place was packed with Americans and other visitors. After five hours, we skipped the last few holes and went to the bar.

You'll hear a lot of great things about Rosses Point if you ask around in

It's no wonder Ireland's greatest poet, William Butler Yeats, wanted his ashes returned to Sligo upon his death.

Ireland. In 2003, *Golf Digest* rated it the eighth-best course in the country. It is a very nice course, I agree, but it's not in the top 10 by any means. In fact, it doesn't make my top 20.

Sligo does have a lot going for it. There are spectacular views of Ben Bulben Mountain, Sligo Bay, and Drumcliff Bay. And there are dramatic elevation changes… and plenty of high grass, especially on the back nine. But there are several things missing that keep it in my third tier of links courses. For one, the uninteresting beginning. For another, the lack of high dunes and valleys you find on courses like Waterville and The European Club. I've played Rosses Point twice in the past five years, and to me it simply doesn't live up to the hype.

The first hole is short and uneventful. So is the second. In fact the first four are rather dull. Number 5 (called The Jump), is great, however,

Sligo's Ben Bulben Mountain makes for one of the most beautiful golf course backdrops in the entire country.

Ireland's Greatest Poem

William Butler Yeats was born in Dublin and became Ireland's most famous poet. His mother came from a wealthy Sligo mill and shipping family. Yeats loved the northwest part of Ireland, particularly Sligo, and once said: "The place that has really influenced my life most is Sligo." He wrote poetry and drama, and won the Nobel Prize for literature in 1923. He died in France, and was buried there, before his remains could be brought back to Sligo, where he wished to spend eternity, "under bare Ben Bulben's head in Drumcliff churchyard." Here is, in my opinion, Yeats' best poem:

When You Are Old
By William Butler Yeats

When you are old and grey and full of sleep,
And nodding by the fire, take down this book,
And slowly read, and dream of the soft look
Your eyes had once, and of their shadows deep;

How many loved your moments of glad grace,
And loved your beauty with love false or true,
But one man loved the pilgrim soul in you,
And loved the sorrows of your changing face;

And bending down beside the glowing bars,
Murmur, a little sadly, how Love fled
And paced upon the mountains overhead
And hid his face amid a crowd of stars.

115

with one of the most elevated tee boxes in the country. You have an extraordinarily wide landing area that lets you take a really big rip. The rest of the front nine is pretty tame.

On the back, however, the course gets much harder—and better. You'll probably shoot five strokes higher on the back than on the front. You must drive the ball straight and long to score well.

Don't think I'm being too hard on this course. It's a great experience. If you like links golf, it's better than almost anything you'll play at home. It's just that it's very often described as one of the best in Ireland, but to me it's not even in the same league as the country's really great courses.

- ■ **What's good:** Great scenery of the bays and mountains. Ben Bulben looms just east of the course. Great clubhouse and bar. There were a half-dozen wind surfers in the ocean almost the entire time we played. The wind here always seems to be up, which makes it harder than it looks. County Sligo is a beautiful and wild area—one of my favorite parts of Ireland. This is where the country's most famous poet, William Butler Yeats, was born and buried.
- ■ **What's not:** The front nine is mostly uneventful, except for the great tee shot from the fifth. The back nine is much harder but the scenery is not as good.

When you get in the high stuff, don't be greedy.
Take a 9-iron or higher and make sure you get out.

■ **Best hole:** 17th hole, an uphill, 455-yard (from the Blues) par-4 you'll be lucky to bogey. Easily the best hole on the course. The second shot on this dogleg left and uphill hole is one of the toughest second shots in the country.

Sligo's front nine is a bit of a let-down, but things pick up on the back. Expect to shoot at least five strokes higher.

Number 15 is a good runner up. It's called In the Gap and, as the name suggests, you have to hit an accurate approach between big dunes. Two traps guard the green.

Sligo Details

PMF Score: 79
Design: 21 out of 30
Challenge: 23 out of 30
Condition: 17 out of 20
19th hole: 18 out of 20
Price: €85 in high season; €73 in low season—weekdays about 20% cheaper.
Length: Blue: 6,602 yards
White: 6,383 yards
Buggies and Trolleys: Both
Tee Times: Any day, with some restrictions. 25% deposit to reserve time. Payment in full 21 days from playing date. Cancel 7 days or more before time, 50% refund. After that, no refund.

County Sligo Golf Club
Rosses Point
Co. Sligo, Ireland
Tel. (353-71) 77171
Fax. 77460
jim@countysligogolfclub.ie
www.countysligogolfclub.ie

St. Patrick's Golf Club

**Maheramagorgan Links
and Tra Mor Links
Founded in 1996
Carrigart, Co. Donegal**

■ What links golf was like before modern maintenance...
■ The course to buy if you want to own an Irish classic...
■ Real links golf for only €20... and more

W ant to know what links golf in Ireland was like before modern and expensive groundskeeping practices?

Then don't miss St. Patrick's Golf Club in Donegal.

Your first indication that St. Patrick's is a different kind of links course is the sign on the side of the road. It's a barely noticeable, hand-painted piece of wood, about two miles outside the town of Carrigart.

From there you wander down a single-lane, dirt-and-gravel, pothole-filled road. You can't go more than about five miles per hour... and I don't know what happens if you meet another car coming the other way—I can't believe two cars can pass without one of them getting stuck in a ditch.

When you get to the course entrance, you'll pass through a metal gate—secured with a padlock when the course is closed. After you've driven about a half-mile, you'll come to a small grassy space behind a sand dune. That's the parking lot, big enough for only a dozen cars or so.

The first tee is on the other side of this giant dune. Look for the little "1st Tee sign" painted on a white two-by-four.

The tee box has no markers to describe the layout of the hole. You have to use the scorecard to figure out which way to go. But even if you do wander onto the wrong hole, don't worry. Odds are you won't be interrupting anyone's round, because you're not likely to see more than a handful of other golfers all day.

There's no clubhouse... no snack bar... no restrooms... no starter's shack... not even a bench or a trashcan. In short, there are literally no facilities on the golf course.

It's just you and 36 holes of spectacular links land. In short, forget business deals, social climbing, and all the luxuries of modern golf—it's just you against the raw elements.

This is links golf in its truest form. And this is how the sport was played for most of the 20th century in Ireland.

St. Patrick's does have trolleys—they're located behind the rusting metal shed (which does house several modern mowers).

St. Patrick's is a different kind of links golf course for sure…

You'll find fairways filled with mushrooms, weeds, and clover—but no bare spots. It all blends together into one big soft and cushy tract.

Greens and fairways appear to be cut about once every week or so. Both are shaggy, and super-slow. You can walk this land all day—your legs will still feel good at the end of your round.

They rely on the honor system here: you have to pay and check in at the Carrigart Hotel in the middle of town, several miles from the course.

We showed up at St. Patrick's in mid-October. The hotel had just closed for the season. It's best to call ahead, because if no one knows you're coming, the gates on the dirt and gravel road may be locked. That's exactly what happened to us when we tried to get in a late-evening round the day we arrived.

On the bright side, St. Patrick's is a great place to play if you want to experience unadulterated links golf, with no one else around. If you care more about the setting and the sights than manicured greens and fairways,

When Nicklaus and Co. are done, St. Patrick's and nearby Rosapenna will probably offer the best four courses in a 10-mile radius in Ireland.

you'll love this place.

St. Patrick's has everything a classic links course should have—high dunes, spectacular views, and dramatic elevation changes.

St. Patrick's is on the other end of the golf course spectrum from the tourist-filled links of Tralee and Waterville and the old-world high-society clubs such as Portmarnock and Portrush. The raw elements are spectacular, but it's completely unrefined.

It's hard to figure out what St. Patrick's owners Dermott Walsh and his son Cormac are doing with the place. They also own the Carrigart Hotel. Locals told me the Carrigart was THE place to stay in Donegal in the 1980s. Today, however, it looks only slightly more inviting than a Motel 6.

But remember, the great Rosapenna Hotel is right around the corner. In fact, only a barbed-wire fence separates the St. Patrick's courses from the Rosapenna links.

St. Patrick's has two full-size links courses. The longer of the two is called Maheramagorgan. It's a lengthy 7,108 yards from the tips. And it plays even longer because there's very little roll on the spongy fairways. Maheramagorgan was designed by Ireland's most famous golf architect, Eddie Hackett, who spent the last working day of his life here, laying sod on the 16th hole, which now bears his name.

The shorter course is called Tra Mor. It's a short links, about 5,800 yards. But Tra Mor is laid out on land that is every bit as spectacular as the longer Maheramagorgan course. Tra Mor is the only links course designed by a woman—Joanne O'Haire.

If you want to experience links golf as it was played on many of Ireland's courses for most of the twentieth century, visit St. Patrick's. It's an experience you will never forget… and one that probably won't be around for long.

This is some of the most spectacular links land in the world. The dunes, sea views, and elevation changes are just amazing.

I bet someday soon someone will come along and offer the Walsh family too much money to refuse. And when this course is modernized and cared for properly, it could easily become one of the 20 best in Ireland.

Maheramagorgan Links

■ **What's good:** Price is great… you can have the whole course to yourself… the natural dunes are amazing… many good holes with dramatic views, turns, and elevations. Completely unpretentious.

- **What's not:** The fuzzy fairways and greens are charming at first, but lose their appeal after you've played a half-dozen holes. The tee boxes need markers to let you know if you are on the right hole, because if you get off track, you might never know it. No clubhouse means you have to go back to town for a drink after your round.
- **Best hole:** The groundskeeper I met told me #16 is the best hole—probably because it's famous for being Eddie Hackett's last. But I liked #15, an uphill dogleg to a green that is surrounded by giant, amphitheater dunes. (There's a great picture of this green on the course's lean website.)

Tra Mor Links

- **What's good:** Price… views are even more spectacular than the Maheramagorgan course because you're much closer to the coast and Sheephaven Bay. It has a handful of spectacular holes. Plays longer than it looks because you get essentially no roll.
- **What's not:** Too short (only 5,822 yards from the tips). Same condition problems as Maheramagorgan course.
- **Best hole:** I did not play much of this course, but #18 gives you a spectacular view from the tee box, and #17 is a good and tough dogleg.

It's not hard to figure out why developers bought St. Patrick's and hired Jack Nicklaus to do the new design.

AS WE WERE GOING TO PRESS: I knew this was going to happen. Just before going to press, the Relton Development group of Dublin bought St. Patrick's, and announced that Jack Nicklaus will re-design the course's 36 holes. Golf course construction began in January 2006. When the project is done, the Resort at St. Patrick's Golf Links will consist of a 5-star luxury hotel, with a spa and complete leisure facilities, to be managed by a "world-renowned international hotel operator." They're also putting in 200 luxury apartments, houses, and shops. The golf course will certainly get better. But it's sad to see the most natural and unpretentious links course in the country become another upscale resort.

St. Patrick's Details

Maheramagorgan Links
PMF Score: 67

Design: 24 out of 30
Challenge: 25 out of 30
Condition: 5 out of 20
19th hole: 13 out of 20 (you have to drive to the hotel)

Tra Mor Links PMF Score: 67

Design: 24 out of 30
Challenge: 25 out of 30
Condition: 5 out of 20
19th hole: 13 out of 20
Price: €25 for either course any day
Length: Maheramagorgan: Blue:

7,108 yards; White, 6,556
Tra Mor; Blue, 5,822; White, 5,071
Buggies and Trolleys: Trolleys only
Tee Times: Any time, any day—just call ahead to make sure they're open.

St. Patrick's Golf Links

Magheramagorgan, Carrigart
Co. Donegal, Ireland
Tel. (353-74) 915-5114
Fax. 915-5250
e-mail: carrigarthotel@ireland.com
www.stpatricksgolflinks.com (Great photos of Eddie Hackett designing original course.)

Strandhill Golf Club

Founded in 1931
Strandhill, Co. Sligo

PMF
69
Score

- What to do when a dog steals your ball...
- A great hole the pros hate...
- An Irish links bargain... and more

D erek McNamara of Connemara Golf Club was waiting for his turn to putt on Strandhill's 7th green.
McNamara was playing in the 2000 Irish Under 18 National Close Boys Championship.

What McNamara didn't know at the time was that a stray dog had snuck onto the course. It wandered around the front nine for a bit before making its way to the 7th hole. There, the dog spotted McNamara and his playing partner on the 7th green. As McNamara looked over the line of his putt, the dog darted full-speed onto the green, scooped up McNamara's ball, and ran off.

There's a great photograph on the clubhouse wall that captures the most exciting part of this event.

If this should ever happen to you, by the way, USGA rules state you can replace your ball without penalty where the original ball came to rest.

Strandhill Golf Club doesn't get much attention or publicity, but it's a very nice links golf course. It's not a top links course by any means, but it is certainly a place where you can have a very enjoyable day of golf.

Strandhill has some

Strandhill could get considerably better in the next few years—they've purchased 60 acres for expansion and redesign.

spectacular views of the crashing Atlantic waves, the Knocknarea Mountain, and the nearby village. Plus, it's a completely unpretentious place, with many decent holes and several that are spectacular.

On the nearby Culleenamore Beach you may see jockeys who still use the hard-packed sand to exercise their horses. This beach is in play on holes #3 and #4. It's not a designated hazard. And it's not out of bounds. You can play from here if you hook one onto the sand.

Number 13 is one of my favorite holes in all of Ireland. It's a 376-yard par-4 called The Valley. From the elevated tee you can't see much of the fairway, which is blocked by a giant dune. There's more fairway here than you think. After this huge dogleg right you have a tough approach shot, between two tall dunes to a tiny green.

Numbers 6 and 7 are great too… and so is #15, a long dogleg left par-4 uphill with a super-steep slope to the green. If you have to play from the sand trap behind the green, you can easily go all the way back down the hill and be farther away than you were before.

Strandhill has spectacular scenery—giant dunes, crashing waves, and the Knocknarea Mountain in the background.

If you want an enjoyable day of links golf where you can score well even without your best game, this is a good place.

Strandhill may get considerably better in the next few years. The club has purchased 60 acres of land to develop four new holes.

Strandhill is a fairly easy course as far as links go—but it's a bargain, with great scenery... the perfect place to spend a golfing afternoon.

- ■ **What's good:** The 13th is one of the best holes in Ireland. Several other great holes too: 6, 7, and 15. Spectacular views of the crashing ocean waves and Knocknarea Mountain. Great clubhouse (it's new) with a restaurant and bar. Good value—only €40 on weekdays. One of Ireland's undiscovered gems.

- ■ **What's not:** If you are a low handicapper, it's pretty easy… and it's missing the characteristic rough and deep bunkers of the traditional full-size links. It's also a little short, measuring only about 6,400 yards from the tips.

- ■ **Best hole:** #13 is blind tee shot par-4 dogleg right where you can't afford to hit it too long. Five-wood or long iron is plenty off the tee. Second shot to a very narrow approach. Big dunes guard a tiny green—this approach is the narrowest in the country. From the tee you have dramatic views of almost the entire course from one of the highest points. Spectacular. This is one of the great quirky links holes in Ireland.

Strandhill Details

PMF Score: 69
Design: 19 out of 30
Challenge: 18 out of 30
Condition: 16 out of 20
19th hole: 16 out of 20
Price: €40 on weekdays
€50 on weekends
Length: Blue: 6,206; White: 6,029
Buggies and Trolleys: Both

Tee Times: Available any day. 50% booking fee. Refund if you cancel with a week's notice or more.

Strandhill Golf Club
Strandhill, Co. Sligo, Ireland
Tel. (353-71) 916-8188
Fax. 916-8811
e-mail: strandhillgc@eircom.net
www.strandhillgc.com

6

The North

D on't be afraid of Northern Ireland. It's safe. Probably a lot safer than where you live in the United States. "The Troubles" between Catholics and Protestants are mostly a thing of the past. And where they do still exist, it's confined to just a few streets in a few towns. As a visitor, you will never be bothered.

The people in the North are just as friendly as those in the South. Most importantly, the golf courses are just as good, although they're generally a bit pricier. Remember, the currency is different in Northern Ireland—they use British Sterling, because this is really part of the United Kingdom, not Ireland. Here's the alphabetical listing of the links courses in Northern Ireland, along with their PMF scores:

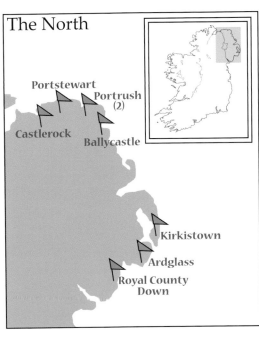

The North

Portstewart
Portrush (2)
Castlerock
Ballycastle
Kirkistown
Ardglass
Royal County Down

COURSE	PMF SCORE	PAGE
Ardglass Golf Club	77	128
Ballycastle Golf Club	55	133
Castlerock Golf Club	68	136
Kirkistown Golf Club	58	139
Portrush Golf Club (Dunluce Links)	89	141
Portrush (Valley Links)	81	141
Portstewart Golf Club	91	146
Royal County Down	91	149

Ardglass Golf Club

Founded in 1896
Ardglass, Co. Down

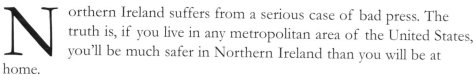

PMF

77

Score

- "The Troubles" in Ireland—3,000 people killed in 25 years...
- The friendliest golf pro in the country...
- Irish Sea hazards... and more

N orthern Ireland suffers from a serious case of bad press. The truth is, if you live in any metropolitan area of the United States, you'll be much safer in Northern Ireland than you will be at home.

"The Troubles," as the problems between the North and South are called, stem from hundreds of years of British rule—and the Irish trying to get them to go home. During most of this occupation, the Brits treated the Irish pretty poorly—they weren't allowed to own land, vote, or even own businesses.

After the War of Irish Independence, the British held onto the northern part of the country, which today is still part of the U.K.

Ever since independence, there have been battles between folks who want to remain part of Britain (mostly Protestants) and other folks who want to be done with British rule (mostly Catholics).

The Irish Republican Army declared a cease-fire in 1994, after a 25-year campaign in which roughly 3,000 people were killed. The Good Friday Agreement of 1998 solidified the peace efforts.

These agreements have played a large role in the peace process, but so have improving economic conditions. Until the past two decades, Northern

Ardglass has the best opening tee box in Irealnd—the ocean to one side, a fourteenth-century building behind you.

128

Ireland thrived, mostly because they had lots of help from Britain. The Republic (South), meanwhile, suffered. There were tens of thousands of unemployed and angry young men running around in Ireland—a sure recipe for violence, bombings, and political "statements."

Then came the "Celtic Tiger"—the nickname for the Republic of Ireland's booming economy. Most young people were finally able to get good jobs. They bought houses and other material goods at a record pace. (For example,

You've lost your ball forever if you don't make Ardglass' chasm-crossing on the 167-yard par-3 #2 called Howd's Hole.

the Irish have more cell phones per person than any other country in the world.) Most people became too busy with their careers to care any longer about the problems in the North.

What most people don't know is that Northern Ireland's economy was booming during the same period. In the 1990s it grew faster than any other region of Britain. In fact, Northern Ireland now has lower unemployment than London and Scotland.

The point is, for the most part, things are good in Ireland, so folks want nothing to do with the conflict.

I got a good taste of Northern Ireland friendliness on my recent trip to Ardglass Golf Club, which is about 45 miles southeast of Belfast.

There I met Phil Farrell, the friendliest golf pro I met on my journey.

When I first called Phil, he told me to come out any time to play his course. Then, when I got there, he asked me if I needed help with any of my arrangements. I explained how I was having a tough time with Royal County Down. Without hesitation, he picked up the phone and helped me arrange a time for the next day. He gave me his card and told me to give him a ring if I had any more problems.

Ardglass Golf Club doesn't get much attention, but it has some of the most spectacular cliff-side holes on the entire island, including a fantastic opener. The first shot is breathtaking—it's an uphill drive with the crashing waves and rocks to the left. Anything left will find the ocean.

Ardglass, like Old Head, is not a true links course… it's more of a cliff-side layout. Missing are the huge dunes and true links turf. But it's worth visiting all the same.

In fact, the first six holes are amazing… played out along the tops of 200-foot cliffs. The Irish Sea and the Mourne Mountains make a great backdrop. You've got to hit it out over the sea and cliffs on several of these holes.

For the first third of the course, you can't wait to see what's next. Then, things settle down into some uneventful interior farmland. It picks up again on the back nine… the 480-yard par-5 11th and the 181-yard par-3 12th are amazing.

This course is worth playing simply because it has a handful of truly spectacular holes. But this is a third-tier course that's unlikely to move up in my rankings unless the interior holes are vastly improved.

The clubhouse has an interesting history. First of all, it looks nothing

It's only a 488-yard par-5, but Ardglass' 11th, called St. John's, is one of the toughest holes on the course. Stray from the fairway and you'll be penalized.

like the modern atrocities you'll find
at so many Irish courses. Parts of
Ardglass clubhouse date back to the
fourteenth century. The building is
listed as a national monument,
which means they can't do much to
alter it. The wall behind the 1st tee
is called the "Ancient Monument."
The cannons in front of the clubhouse date to the fifteenth century.

■ **What's good:** The incredible
scenery—some of the best in
Ireland. This is a truly enjoyable

*The finishing hole at Ardglass—a great view of the
clubhouse, sea, and first few holes.*

place to play. Great and friendly welcome... attractive clubhouse with fifteenth-
century cannons lining the front. The course settles down after the first six
holes... then begins to pick up again a few holes later, with more holes that
overlook the water and the coast. It has fantastic tee boxes... seven or eight of
them are elevated and offer dramatic views of the sea. If you bring a camera,
you'll find yourself pulling it out of the bag on at least 10 holes. The layout is
wide open, which makes it a nice place for the average golfer. You don't have
to be very long or accurate to have a great time and score well here. The greens
are fast and mostly true. Great photographs on the website. A real bargain by
Northern Ireland's standards.

Ardglass doesn't get much attention, but it has several holes that are as dramatic as any in the country.

■ **What's not:** Not a true links test. There's little in the way of high marram grass that links courses are famous for. Very hilly course to walk… no buggies allowed. You don't have the narrow drives and dangerous approaches of a true links classic course.

■ **Best hole:** #4 is a short but spectacular 365-yard par-4, with a narrow fairway, and cliffs and ocean to the left. But my favorite was #11, a short 488-yard par-5 that goes left to right. You have to hit your tee shot out over the water, and there's not much room for a safe landing. See photo earlier in chapter.

Ardglass Details

PMF Score: 77

Design: 22 out of 30
Challenge: 21 out of 30
Condition: 16 out of 20
19th hole: 18 out of 20

Price: £32 on weekdays
£45 on weekends

Length: White: 6,258 yards
Green: 5,819 yards

Buggies and Trolleys: Trolleys only. No buggies allowed.

Tee Times: Any day, but Saturdays are very busy. Sundays only after 12:30. 25% deposit required. Cancel more than one week out, no additional charge; less than one week, 50% charge.

Ardglass Golf Club

Castle Place, Ardglass
Northern Ireland
BT30 7TP
Tel. 44-28-44-841022
e-mail: info@ardglassgolfclub.com
www.ardglassgolfclub.com

Ballycastle Golf Club

PMF 55 Score

Founded in 1893
Ballycastle, Co. Antrim

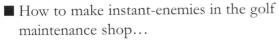

- How to make instant-enemies in the golf maintenance shop…
- A twelfth-century religious hazard… and more

"**A**re those guys sleeping on the green?" I asked.

"I think so," Mark replied.

Up ahead, four grown men were stretched out on the par-5, 495-yard 12th green.

A protest, I wondered? A new way for Irish environmentalists to stop golf-course construction?

As we got closer, we could see these guys were not sleeping. Instead, they were each stretched out on their own large piece of plastic and were removing blades of grass, one at a time, from the green.

"What's going on?" I asked

"Yer man used de wrong seed," replied a curly-haired, early-40s fellow.

Turns out someone on the grounds crew staff used the wrong seed on two of Ballycastle Golf Club's greens.

These four unlucky fellows were removing each blade by hand… thousands of pieces in all on each green.

We sidestepped the four Irish lads and continued our round at one of the oldest golf clubs in Ireland.

Ballycastle Golf Club is a hybrid course… part parkland, part links. The first five holes are played across Cushendall Road,

The first few holes at Ballycastle are a real letdown—except for the twelfth-century Bonamargy Abbey between the 2nd and 3rd.

along the banks of the Margy and Carey Rivers. It's a disappointing parkland beginning that's completely uneventful except for the ruins of the twelfth-century Bonamargy Abbey between the second and third holes.

The course picks up considerably on #6 when you cross the road again and begin playing along the coast. You have some nice views of the Mull of Kintyre, Rathlin Island, and Ballycastle Bay. There's no high grass or dunes to speak of. It's more of a cliff-side course than a true links layout, but there are a few great holes.

■ **What's good:** #9 is great... so is #17—some of the biggest elevation changes I've ever seen on a golf course. Ballycastle is "links lite"—good for the high handicapper. You can hit it all over the place and still not lose a ball. It's cheap, and the people are friendly and welcoming.

Ballycastle's downhill par-3 17th.

The best hole at Ballycastle is #9, The Dooans, pictured here. You play over a green off the tee to an elevated green. This is a wild hole. It's only about 360 yards from the tips.

■ What's not:

Mostly an unimaginative design, except for a few spectacular holes. Not a true links experience. First five holes are a big letdown, and need to be redesigned.

Only in the British Isles will you find twelfth-century ruins right next to a golf course. Pictured here: Bonamargy Abbey

■ Best hole:

#9, The Dooans. This is a wild hole. It's only about 360 yards from the tips. From the tee you have a huge landing area, part of which takes you over the 17th green. Use an iron, but get as close as you can to the hill that leads to the green. Your second shot is a super-tough uphill approach to a small green that's at least 100 feet above the fairway. There's very little room for error. And it's much better to be short than long, as we learned the hard way.

Ballycastle Details

PMF Score: 55
Design: 13 out of 30
Challenge: 12 out of 30
Condition: 15 out of 20
19th hole: 15 out of 20
Price: £20 weekdays
      £30 on weekends
Length: White: 5,927 yards
      Green: 5,744 yards
Trolleys and Buggies: Trolleys only

Tee times: No restrictions except for competition days. No deposit required.

Ballycastle Golf Club

Cushendall Road, Ballycastle,
Co. Antrim
Northern Ireland, BT54 6QP
Tel. (44 28) 207-62506
e-mail: Use form on website
www.ballycastlegolfclub.com

Castlerock Golf Club

Founded in 1901
Castlerock, Co. Londonderry

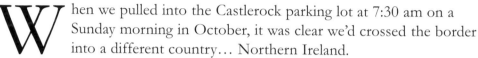

PMF
68
Score

- How the Protestant work ethic will affect your golf game...
- The second most-crowded course in the country...
- My favorite tee-time system in Ireland... and more

When we pulled into the Castlerock parking lot at 7:30 am on a Sunday morning in October, it was clear we'd crossed the border into a different country... Northern Ireland.

Nowhere on our trip had we seen more than a half-dozen cars when we arrived at a golf course at the crack of dawn. In fact, many courses in Ireland even give you a discount if you play before 8 am.

But Castlerock was packed.

Castlerock, of course, *is* in a different country—Northern Ireland... part of the U.K. Is it the Protestant work ethic that makes the Northern Irish more likely to get up so early in the morning to play golf? I don't know.

I do know that I loved Castlerock's tee-time system.

There were no pre-bookings. No time sheets. No starters. Instead,

The Irish in the Republic don't generally like early tee times. But it's a different story at Castlerock.

136

there's a simple metal chute that keeps everything in order. You drop in your ball, and when it appears at the other end, it's your turn on the tee. First-come, first-served.

We played the course in mid-October, so maybe it's not this simple in the prime months.

Castlerock is a decent but not great links course. I rank it in the fourth tier. It's better than most courses in the United States, but certainly not one of the top links in Ireland. It was, however, very crowded—more crowded than any other course we played, except perhaps for Sligo.

Castlerock actually has 27 holes. We played the 18 that make up the "championship" Mussenden Course. As was the case at Connemara, the extra nine (called the Bann Course) looked more exciting than the "championship" links. The Bann Course seems to have more dunes, which line the fairways and guard the greens.

If I play the course again, I'll try the Bann Course and skip one of the other nines. The Bann course, however, is very short… just 2,446 yards from the tips.

■ **What's good:** The train tracks that run right next to the course on numbers 3, 4, and 5… several spectacular holes on the short Bann Course… good introduction to links golf… a course that's not too hard for high handicappers.

Castlerock is a decent, but not great links course. It ranks in my fourth tier, but is still better than most non-links courses.

■ **What's not:** Not a true links challenge—there's very little high grass and not enough challenge from the tees… it was very crowded, especially for October… weekends are pricey for a course that's not a top links challenge.

■ **Best hole:** #8 on the Mussenden Course is a 411-yard (from the tips) par-4, which doglegs hard to the right. It's a difficult hole to drive… and a good challenge. #5 par-5 on the Bann Course.

Castlerock is an "everyman's" links. When we played it on a Saturday in October, the place was packed all day long.

Castlerock Details

PMF Score: 68
Design: 19 out of 30
Challenge: 18 out of 30
Condition: 15 out of 20
19th hole: 16 out of 20
Price: £50 on weekdays
£70 on weekends
Length: Blue: 6,747 yards
White: 6,506 yards
Buggies and Trolleys: Both

Tee Times: 25% non-refundable deposit required to book times.

Castlerock Golf Club
65 Circular Road, Castlerock
Co. Londonderry, Northern Ireland
Tel. (44-28) 7084-8314
Fax. 7084-9440
e-mail: info@castlerockgc.co.uk
www.castlerockgc.co.uk

Kirkistown Golf Club

Founded in 1902
Cloughey, Co. Down

■ A golf course that helped the Allies win WWII
■ A trolley and scorecard waiting for you in the
   morning... and more

K irkistown Castle Golf Club has two problems.
   One: It's not a very good golf course.
   Two: It's a long way from anything else—near the small town of
Cloughey, on the Ards Peninsula. From the south you have to take a ferry...
and from the north it's a long, long drive on highway A2 from Belfast.

It has a few very good holes, and it's quite cheap, but this is not what
you're looking for if you've traveled across the Atlantic Ocean to play
links golf.

The place does have some interesting history. In 1941, during World
War II, locals took sand and gravel from the course to build airfields at
Kirkistown and Ballyhalbert. You can still see the depressions in the ground
in front of the first tee and behind the 3rd green.

■ **What's good:** It's cheap... and it's easy, even for high handicappers... #2 and
#10 are great
holes with dra-
matic elevations
to tricky greens...
the people here
are very friend-
ly—they left out
two trolleys and
scorecards for us
to play early in
the morning
before any course
employees

*Kirkistown has a few interesting holes. But it's not worth traveling too far
out of your way to play.*

arrived. I guess the Protestant work ethic doesn't apply here.

The folks running the pro shop left pull carts and scorecards for us so we could tee off before the staff arrived. Where else in the world does that happen?

- ■ **What's not:** The holes are very close together... the course is wide open... not a true test of links golf... far away from almost everything else. Unremarkable course that's worth playing only if you are nearby.

- ■ **Best hole:** #2 and #10 are similar. Tough par-4s with narrow approaches to uphill and elevated greens. Number 12 is good too... a long par-4 that is uphill to an elevated green near a centuries-old building that sits in ruins.

Kirkistown Details

PMF Score: 58

Design: 16 out of 30
Challenge: 16 out of 30
Condition: 11 out of 20
19th hole: 15 out of 20
Price: £25 on weekdays
         £30 on weekends
Length: White: 6,146 yards
Buggies and Trolleys: Trolleys only

Tee Times: No restrictions or deposits required.

Kirkistown Castle Golf Club

142 Main Road, Cloughey
Newtownards, Co. Down
Northern Ireland, BT22-1JA
Tel. (44-28) 4277-1233
Fax. 4277-1699
e-mail: kirkistown@supanet.com
www.linksgolfkirkistown.com

Royal Portrush Golf Club

Dunluce and Valley Links
Founded in 1888
Portrush, Co. Antrim

- Three great golf courses, within a 10-mile radius…
- Site of the 2005 and 2007 Senior British Open…
- Don't forget your knee-high socks… and more

K enny McClinton pulled a gun from his pocket.
The bus drivers needed to be taught a lesson.
Militant Protestant leaders had called for a strike, but the bus drivers weren't listening. So a leader of the group, James Pratt Craig, called upon one of his hit men, Kenny McClinton. The task: Kill a bus driver in Protestant West Belfast. It didn't matter if it was a Catholic or a Protestant… but odds were, in this part of town, it would be a Protestant.

So McClinton boarded a bus on Crumlin Road on an overcast summer day.

He stepped on, and walked up to Harry Bradshaw, the driver. McClinton never pulled any money from his pocket to pay the fare— instead he reached for his gun, looked Bradshaw in the eyes, and shot him in the head at point-blank range. McClinton calmly walked off the bus, covered in Bradshaw's blood.

James Pratt Craig's Protestant group wrote a letter of apology to Sheila Bradshaw, the bus driver's

This is one of the great par-3s in Irealnd—Portrush's #14 called Calamity. Don't miss right.

wife. They enclosed a £10 bill... and said they thought Bradshaw was Catholic.

This took place in the summer of 1977. When you hear stories like this, it's no wonder Americans (as well as Irish, British, and most of the rest of the world) were—and in many cases, still are—afraid to go to Northern Ireland.

But the truth is, Northern Ireland is now a very safe place.

And it's a shame more Americans—especially golfers—don't visit, because three of the country's best courses are here. One of these courses is Portrush Golf Club (the other two are Portstewart and Royal County Down). Portrush actually has two courses: the "championship" Dunluce course, and the newer Valley course.

Portrush is one of the most famous and well-regarded courses in Ireland.

It hosted the first Irish Amateur Championship in 1892... the Irish Open... the Women's British Open...

On the 448-yard 17th, stay left to avoid "Big Bertha," one of the biggest bunkers in Ireland.

and was the first and only Irish course to host the British Open, back in 1951. (Remember, Northern Ireland is officially part of Britain, not Ireland.) In all, the course has hosted more than 50 Irish and British championships. The Senior Men's British Open was here in 2004 and 2005 and will be back in 2007.

Does it deserve its lofty reputation? Yes... but...

It is a very nice course, no doubt. But I believe Portrush is a bit over-rated. It is simply not in the same league as The European Club, Waterville, and the rest of Ireland's top five.

The main drawback is that the course is played up on a hill, away from the coast. You are separated from the sea and giant dunes by the Valley Links. (The closest you get is the 5th green and 6th tee.) Don't get me wrong, this is a spectacular course, worth going well out of your way to play. But practically every golf publication in the world ranks Portrush among Ireland's top three links courses. It simply does not belong there.

How does the Valley course compare with the Dunluce links?

The views are certainly better on the Dunluce course—you can see the ocean from almost every hole. The Valley is—as the name indicates—in a valley between the Dunluce course and the sea. The Dunluce course is longer too, by about 500 yards from the blue tees... and 600 yards from the whites. But other than that... the courses are comparable. If you can play only one, choose the Dunluce, but you shouldn't lose any sleep over the fact that you might have to settle for the Valley.

Portrush and Portstewart are only about 10 minutes from each other. That gives you three of Ireland's top 20 within a 20-mile radius.

One more thing: Don't forget your knee-high socks. The official course policy dictates that if you wear shorts you must also wear knee-length socks.

Photo: Mark Fost

Portrush is the only Irish course to host the British Open—and regularly hosts the Senior's Open.

Dunluce Links

■ **What's good:** This is a top-15 links course for sure, in as good a shape as any we played… plenty of elevated tee shots. Great views of the sea. Look for the "Big Bertha" sand trap on #17—it's the deepest sand trap I've ever seen, and will gobble up a sliced tee shot. The members and employees are very friendly here. It's the site of three Senior's British Opens between 2004 and 2007. Has one of the most famous par-3s in the country—#14, a 202-yard hole called Calamity. Anything short or right finds a huge chasm, and a high score. Every par-4 and -5 except #s 1 and 18 are doglegs. A great place to show someone a top links course in nearly perfect condition.

■ **What's not:** The design and length are tough—but it's not awe-inspiring like most of the courses in Ireland's top 10. No yardage markers, so you need a stroke saver or a caddie, for sure. Most of the Valley course sits between the Dunluce course and the sea, which means on the Dunluce you never get close to the ocean and the giant seaside dunes.

■ **Best hole:** #14 Calamity is the most famous hole, but I like #5 (called White Rocks). It's only 379 yards from the white tees, but it's a hole that gives you options. It's a blind tee-shot over a big mound, and a dogleg to the right.

The Dunluce links at Portrush gets all the attention, but the Valley links is almost as good. Two great links in one spot.

You're tempted to cut off as much of the dogleg as possible... but you've got to hit it a long way to do so. This green is the closest you will get to the water. Hit your approach too far and you'll land in the sea.

Valley Links

- ■ **What's good:** Located in the valley between the Dunluce course and the sea, this course puts you closer to the water and the tremendous dunes... but never puts you in the high dunes. Cheaper than the Dunluce links... and almost as good. Shorter than Dunluce—which is good for folks who don't hit it very far. This is a second-tier links in great condition. Real bargain at £40.

- ■ **What's not:** Considerably shorter than the Dunluce course at just over 6,000 yards from the white tees. Not many memorable holes.

- ■ **Best hole:** A 400-yard par-4, #8 is a great links hole. You have to drive the ball into a long and narrow fairway between two sand dunes. Then, the green is at the end of another long and narrow valley.

Portrush Details

Dunluce Links PMF Score: 89

Design: 26 out of 30
Challenge: 26 out of 30
Condition: 19 out of 20
19th hole: 18 out of 20
Price: £105 weekdays; £120 week-ends; (Nov. to March is only £60; excluding Sat.)
Length: Blue: 6,845 yards
      White: 6,641 yards
Buggies and Trolleys: Trolleys, but no buggies. Caddies if you call in advance.
Tee Times: Tee times are available every day of the week, with restrictions. You must pay a £50 non-refundable deposit in advance, and must pay the entire balance two months before your time.

Valley Links PMF Score: 81

Design: 23 out of 30
Challenge: 23 out 30
Condition: 18 out of 20
19th hole: 17 out of 20
Price: £35 weekdays; £40 weekends; (Nov. to March is only £25; excluding Sat.)
Length: Blue: 6,304 yards
      White: 6,054 yards
Buggies and Trolleys: Trolleys only; caddies if you call in advance.
Tee Times: Same as Dunluce.

Portrush Golf Club

Dunluce Road, Portrush
Co. Antrim, Northern Ireland,
BT56 8JQ
Tel. (44-28) 7082-2311
Fax. 70823139
info@royalportrushgolfclub.com
www.royalportrushgolfclub.com

Portstewart Golf Club

Founded in 1894
Portstewart, Co. Londonderry

PMF
91
Score

- ■ A Northern Ireland bargain…
- ■ The secret behind why the Irish play so fast…
- ■ The best opening hole in the country… and more

O n Portstewart's first tee, I glanced over my shoulder and saw a group of ladies heading our way.

No problem, I thought.

Certainly three guys in their early 30s could play faster than three 60-something Irish women, right?

Well, we found a lot of trouble on Portstewart's fantastic first hole—undoubtedly the best opening hole in the country. And the old ladies from the North were right on our tails. They stared us down with arms crossed and knickers flapping in the breeze.

On the second tee, the women had to wait for us again. We decided to pick up the pace, determined to put some distance between us. On the fourth I thought we'd done it… but they turned up on the tee just as I was about to hit my approach. We had to literally jog the rest of the fourth hole to lose them.

We weren't playing slow—not by American standards, anyway. But these ladies were flying—like all Irish golfers do.

It's one of the great things about Irish golf—the people in this country play at least twenty five percent faster than we do. Old, young, Northern, Southern, men, women, and children… they all play fast. A regular round takes four hours… a fast round takes three and a half hours.

The reason?

I believe it's because the Irish are used to playing in rot-

The front nine at Portstewart is unbelievable—arguably the best front nine in the country. Pictured here: #2.

ten weather. On a cold and rainy day you want to hit the ball as quickly as possible, keep moving, and get back to the clubhouse fast. As Paul Daley says in *The Lure of the Links*, "You must walk briskly on the links, not only to avoid slow play but as a requirement to prevent your blood from icing over. When the coastal squalls start to kick in, the links are no place to dawdle."

On my recent trip, we played Portstewart on beautiful sunny afternoon. The Irish women behind us kept the pressure on all day.

Portstewart is an under-rated course. It's one of the 10 best in the entire country. The front nine, in fact, is as good as any nine holes I've ever played. Probably the best front nine in all of Ireland. Put it with Tralee's back nine, and you'd have the country's best links course.

Sandwiched between the River Bann and the rolling Atlantic Ocean, Portstewart's tract guides you in and out and up and down... over huge dunes and giant elevations... into deep valleys and around heavy gorse (spiny shrubs). You have spectacular sea views along the way. All nine holes on the front side are very, very good.

But then... the course changes dramatically on the back.

You'll feel like you've made a wrong turn... like you got sidetracked onto a different course.

The back nine is mostly wide open, much easier, and much less interest-

At just £65 during the week, Portstewart is the best links deal in Northern Ireland—half the price of some of the more famous courses.

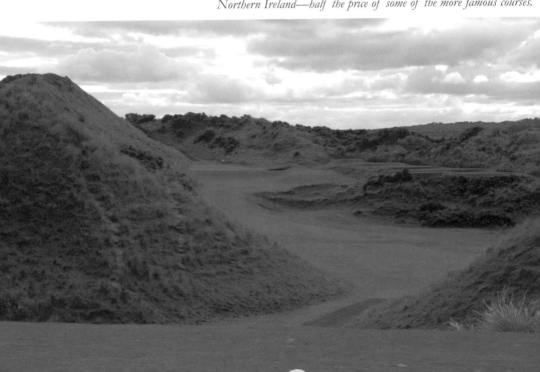

ing. In fact, it's tough to give Portstewart an overall score, because the front nine is so much better than the back. I'd like to see the nines switched... or intermingled, so you don't have to play all of the great holes in the beginning. Still, even with nine mediocre back-nine holes, Portstewart is one of Ireland's 10 best, which shows you just how good the front nine is.

Portstewart actually has three 18-hole courses. The best, and the only full-sized layout is the Strand Course. The River Course is just 5,700 yards, and the Old Course is about 1,000 yards shorter than the River.

- ■ **What's good:** Front nine is as good as any in the country... dunes, views, and design are spectacular. You get the full links experience in just nine holes. Town of Portstewart has plenty of decent accommodations, good pubs, and decent restaurants. The course is cheaper than nearby Portrush—and even with a mediocre back nine, a better golf experience. Try the high-pressure air guns to clean your cleats after your round.

- ■ **What's not:** Not well marked. We didn't have a Strokesaver guide or a caddie, and it was very difficult to judge distances. There is just one marker on each hole—a small yellow triangle at 150 yards in the middle of the fairway. With so many dunes and undulations, distances are deceiving. Back nine is a big letdown after the spectacular front.

- ■ **Best hole:** So many good ones it's hard to choose. #1 is great... so is #4, but #7 is probably the best hole on the course. It's a 516-yard par-5 from the blue tees, uphill, surrounded on both sides by giant dunes.

Portstewart Details

PMF Score: 91

Design: 28 out of 30
Challenge: 27 out of 30
Condition 18 out of 20
19th hole: 18 out of 20
Price: £65 weekdays; £85 weekends
Length: Blue: 6,895 yards
White: 6,571 yards
Buggies and Trolleys: Both
Tee Times: Wednesdays and Saturdays are women's and men's competition days. Few times available for visitors. Sundays are limited also, but other days are not. You must make full payment one month in advance. 75% refund with "proper notification."

Portstewart Golf Club

117 Strand Rd, Portstewart
Co. Londonderry, Northern Ireland, BT557PG
Tel. (44-28) 708-32015
Fax. 708-34097
e-mail: bill@portstewartgc.co.uk
www.portstewartgc.co.uk

Royal County Down Golf Club

Founded in 1889
Newcastle, Co. Down

PMF
91
Score

- The man who knows the course best has never played it…
- The 10th best course in the world?…
- The most photographed hole in Ireland, and more

Most of the golf courses built in Ireland in the late 1800s follow a similar timeline…

They were constructed by British Aristocracy or the military. For several generations, British "gentlemen" played in waistcoats and bow ties… ladies in corsets and long dresses. The local (and very poor) Irish were not allowed to play—instead they worked. They staffed the restaurants and hotels, and carried members' bags (often barefoot). They were certainly never allowed to walk through the clubhouse front door.

Then, over the next 100 years—thanks to Irish independence, decades of poverty, emigration, and an economy that went nowhere—golf in Ireland became an "everyman's" game.

Today, because of a booming Irish economy and hundreds of thousands of overseas visitors, most Irish courses are doing quite well. And locals can join almost any course they want, by paying just a few hundred Euros a year.

But a few courses have held on to the exclusivity of the aristocratic years gone by. And no one does a better job of putting on pretentious airs than Royal County Down (RCD), in Northern Ireland. You can't join RCD on your own, no matter how much money you have.

You definitely want a caddie for Royal County Down— lots of blind tee shots and second shots.

149

You have to be invited by a current member.

There's a level of pretense here you just don't find elsewhere in Ireland. The folks running Royal County Down were hesitant to let us play. But I insisted, because I'd heard it was the best course in Ireland.

Yes, the folks here are a bit pretentious... but Royal County Down is well worth going out of your way to play.

Everywhere else in the world, exclusive private golf clubs are the norm. But in Ireland, it seems strange. Of course, you have to keep it all in perspective…

If this course was in the United States, you wouldn't even be allowed up the private driveway. But remember in Ireland—even in the British North—every course, no matter how old and exclusive, is open to the public.

Even though you can't play every day of the week, and even though you can't use the members-only clubhouse (they're building a new one for visitors), these small inconveniences are trivial and quickly forgotten once you step onto one of the world's truly great links golf courses.

We played Royal County Down on an overcast but warm day in October, with a fantastic caddie named Mick, who's been here for 27 years. (Although Mick knows the course as well as anyone in the world, he's never played it himself. Caddies aren't allowed.)

Royal County Down is indeed a very nice course. It's clearly one of the 10 best in the country.

And most critics rank the course even higher than I do. *Golf Digest's* 2003 rankings list RCD as the second best course in Ireland after Royal Portrush. *Golf Magazine's* 2003 ratings say it's the 10th-best course in the entire world. These folks obviously have not played all of the other great courses in Ireland. To me the reputation is slightly better than the course.

Don't misunderstand me. RCD is a beautiful place, famous for the flowering gorse and heather that line the fairways. And if you don't hit it straight here, you'll have a very rough day. The dunes and the views are magnificent.

RCD has everything you could want in a top links course. It's a magnificent location—at the foothill of the Mourne Mountains, with the elegant Slieve Donard Hotel in the backdrop. Number nine (on the cover of this book) is probably the most photographed hole in the entire country.

RCD regularly hosts the Walker Cup (next in 2007). This would be a great tournament to attend, in a great setting.

RCD is long and tough… and in excellent shape. If only the people who run the place would lighten up a bit.

■ **What's good:** It's a top-notch links test, the best in the North. Definitely better than Portrush, and better than Portstewart only because Portstewart's back nine is so week. There aren't any holes at RCD that take your breath away, like Tralee or Waterville, but every hole is a real links challenge. Great caddie… and RCD has a

The most famous, most photographed, and best hole at Royal Country Down, the par-4, 425-yard 9th.

great history. Many pros play this course before the British Open. Tiger and friends sometimes fly in by helicopter. RCD has some of the best bunkers in the country, with really high grass at the lip, which adds an extra challenge. (Doonbeg and Whistling Straights in the U.S. have copied this feature.) Good pro shop too, but expensive. RCD is hosting the Walker Cup in 2007, the amateur version of Ryder Cup.

Photo: Mark Fost

The tee shot from the famous 9th, with the spire of the Slieve Donard Hotel in the background.

- **What's not:** You definitely need a caddie to play this course because there are so many blind tee shots; £30 per bag plus tip. Snootiness of the club is a turnoff, especially after being welcomed so warmly almost everywhere else you go. The small pond on #17 is ridiculous, and should be removed.

- **Best hole:** #9 is a 425-yard par-4 (486 from the back tees) with a blind tee shot, then a 50-foot drop in elevation—a good drive carries this drop. Then you have a valley-like fairway with the Slieve Donard Hotel in the background. Two bunkers guard the green, which is very sloped.

Royal County Down Details

PMF Score: 91
Design: 27 out of 30
Challenge: 28 out of 30
Condition: 20 out of 20
19th hole: 16 out of 20
Price: £125 on weekdays; £140 on weekends (it's less than half price November to March)
Length: Blue: 7,065 yards
White: 6,740 yards
Buggies and Trolleys: Trolleys and caddies only, no buggies.
Tee Times: Visitors can't play Wednesday or Saturday, limited times other days. Pay full green fees at least 30 days advance. Cancel more than 30 days out, receive 100% refund; 15-30 days out, 50% refund; less than 15 days, 25% refund.

Royal Country Down Golf Club
36 Golf Links Rd., Newcastle
Co. Down, Northern Ireland
BT330AN
Tel. (44-28) 4372-2419
Fax. 4372-3847
proshop@royalcountydowngolfclub.com
www.royalcountydown.org

7

The East

F ew Americans go to the Ireland's east coast to play golf. But the region has two of the country's best links golf courses—The European Club (my favorite overall) and The Island. The downside is that these are the only two courses in the East that make my top 20. Portmarnock is the most famous course in the region—it's hosted dozens of big tournaments, and makes most critics' top-five list. (It's 23rd on mine). If you go to the east coast specifically to play golf, consider staying in Malahide to avoid Dublin's traffic. Dublin, of course, is a great city—one of the best capitals in Europe. The Island is the best course near Dublin. If you get anywhere near The European Club, make the journey (90 minutes south). Here are Ireland's east coast links courses in alphabetical order.

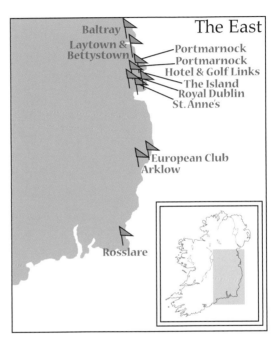

COURSE	PMF SCORE	PAGE
Arklow Golf Club	64	154
County Louth Golf Club (Baltray)	76	157
The European Club	96	160
The Island Golf Club	90	166
Laytown & Bettystown Golf Club	74	170
Portmarnock Golf Club	78	173
Portmarnock Hotel & Golf Links	66	178
Rosslare Golf Club	66	182
Royal Dublin Golf Club	65	186
St. Anne's Golf Club	72	190

Arklow Golf Club

Founded in 1926
Arklow, Co. Wicklow

PMF
64
Score

- Military executions by the 15th green…
- The 2nd-best clubhouse view in the country…
- A golf course (without bunkers) for £2,000…
  and more

To the side of the green on Arklow Golf Club's 15th hole, there's a 12-foot rock that's been the site of many deaths.

This hole is called Sly's Gallows, because this giant rock was once used by a British commander named Sly, who liked to use it as a place to carry out his hangings.

You see, the grounds where Arklow Golf Club sits today have seen their fair share of battles. This land that was once bogs and forest is where several Irish Rebellion battles against the British took place in the late sixteenth century.

During the nineteenth century, the land where the course now stands was owned by the First Earl of Carysfort, Granville Proby, who sold the site to the golf club for £250. To build the course locals hired the firm of Taylor and Hawtree. Taylor was a 5-time British Open Champion.

The firm estimated complete course construction would cost £2,000. When the club and locals couldn't raise that much money, they thought about building just nine holes, and adding nine later. Ultimately they decided to instead have the British firm build a full 18—but without

You won't find a warmer welcome than the one you'll get at Arklow Golf Club, 45 miles south of Dublin.

154

any bunkers to reduce the fee. The course opened for play in 1928.

On my recent trip, I played Arklow with two long-standing members. Eddie and Paddy love their course, live nearby, and play several times a week.

Arklow has a funny layout. Par for the front nine is only 33... and for the back it's 36. The front has no par-5s and three par-3s. The shorter-than-average length of 6,400 yards from the back tees is deceiving, however, because the course is not short. Instead, it's just missing two par-5s. In other words, the average hole lengths are not short at all. There are 7 par-4s over 400 yards, and three of the par-3s are more than 180 yards.

If you play Arklow, I recommend you play it from the tips—it's a good challenge from there.

■ **What's good:** Arklow is a nice introduction to links golf, with a lot to like. However, it is not one of Ireland's great courses. The clubhouse has the second-best view of any in the country (only Old Head's is better). The Arklow clubhouse sits atop a high cliff overlooking the entire course and the Irish Sea. In the distance, several miles from shore, you'll see recently installed wind turbines, which according to my playing partners are 80 meters from tip to tip, and dwarf any passing ship. The price is good... as is the welcome from members, who encourage you to stick around after your round for a pint and something to eat. Good elevated tees on #1, #4, and a few others. Play it from the back tees and it's plenty long.

■ **What's not:** There's just not much room on this stretch of land for a golf

Arklow's best hole, the par-4 14th, called Sly's Gallow. Commander Sly hung prisoners from the rock left of the green.

course. The holes are close together, and you can easily cross an adjacent fairway with a wayward tee shot. The sad part is that the amount of available land is even less now than it was years ago. Beach erosion has washed away

Arklow's clubhouse, which is more elevated than this shot, offers the second-best view of any clubhouse in Ireland (Old Head's is better).

several acres at least. You don't get the true links experience at Arklow—there's little in the way of high grass or big dunes. There aren't many views of the sea except from the clubhouse and a few tee boxes. No pro shop.

■ **Best hole:** Sly's Gallow, par-4 #15 with a little pond you must carry to reach the green. You need two great shots to get home in two, especially if the wind is in your face.

Arklow Details

PMF Score: 64
Design: 17 out of 30
Challenge: 16 out of 30
Condition: 14 out of 20
19th hole: 17 out of 20
Price: €40 on weekdays
€42 on weekends
Length: White (tips): 6,386 yards
Green: 5,969 yards
Buggies and Trolleys: Trolleys and a few buggies (new in 2005).

Tee Times: Limited times on Sundays, all other days OK. No deposit required.

Arklow Golf Club
Abbeylands, Arklow
Co. Wicklow, Ireland
Tel. (353-402) 32492
arklowgolflinks@eircom.net
www.arklowgolflinks.com

County Louth Golf Club

Founded in 1892
Baltray, Co. Louth

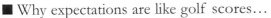

- Why expectations are like golf scores...
- Site of the 2004 Irish Open...
- One of the seven best in Ireland?... and more

E xpectations are like golf scores... the lower they are, the happier you'll be.

I was expecting great things at County Louth Golf Club. The place is also called Baltray, and is about 45 minutes north of Dublin, near the town of Drogheda.

Before my trip, I watched the Irish Open on television, which was held here in the summer of 2004. *Golf Digest* rated the course in its top 100 in the world. A "hidden gem," they called it. The November 2003 issue of *Golf Digest* rated this course the seventh best in Ireland, ahead of classics such as The European Club, Tralee, Enniscrone, The Island, and Portstewart.

So when we pulled into the parking lot, I couldn't wait to see the place.

The bad news is, I was generally disappointed.

Don't get me wrong. This is a nice course. It's a real links challenge. The greens were fantastic, there was plenty of high grass. By regular golf course standards, it is fantastic. But by Irish links standards it is just mediocre.

For me, Baltray is not one of Ireland's top-10 links courses... it's not even one of the top 25.

What's wrong with the place? After all, it does have plenty of length... it is chal-

You'll often see critics rate County Louth one of Ireland's 10-best links. It hosted the 2004 Irish Open.

lenging… and it has lots of high grass typical of a links course. The members are friendly and welcoming, for sure, and the course has hosted the East of Ireland Championship (one of the most prestigious tournaments in the country for amateurs) since 1941.

Well, the way I see it, the main problem is that there's nothing truly memorable about the place. No spectacular views… no giant dunes or dramatic elevation changes… nothing unique or startling. It's just a nice course… not one that takes your breath away as so many great Irish links do.

What this course needs is a makeover (Pat Ruddy: are you listening?) if it wants to move into the top-20 links courses in the country. The course opened in 1892, but the design hasn't been touched since 1937, when British architect Tom Simpson reworked every hole but the fourth.

■ **What's good:** Great welcome… a true links test that held the Irish Open in 2004 and hosts the East Irish Championship each year… slick and undulating greens are very, very good—some of the best of Ireland… lots of dunes, but none that are dramatic… many well-placed bunkers. The course opens with some rather tame holes, but gets good on #12. Numbers 16 and 17 are very good too. The greens were in spectacular condition. The clubhouse doubles as a 12-room hotel, which allows you to be on the course 30 minutes or less after your morning alarm goes off.

■ **What's not:** Baltray was, overall, disappointing. I was expecting a real links

The greens at County Louth are some of the best in Ireland, but to me the course is not remarkable enough to rank anywhere near the top 10.

masterpiece. But it's flat, and there are no unique or imaginative holes. No breathtaking views or spectacular scenery. Still, this is a good links course in top condition, and if you want a real links test it's worth playing. No views of the ocean. There's

At €130 on the weekends, County Louth is one of the most overpriced courses in the country.

nothing to really dislike, but it's not the kind of course you want to rush to play again. Expensive for a course that's not in my top two tiers. One of the most overpriced courses in the country on weekends.

■ **Best hole:** I liked the par-4 410-yard 12th hole—a very good dogleg. Another very good hole is #14. It's a short hole with a fantastic green—I counted five different levels of undulation. One of the most challenging greens I've ever seen.

County Louth Details

PMF Score: 76
Design: 21 out of 30
Challenge: 22 out of 30
Condition: 18 out of 20
19th hole: 15 out of 20
Price: €110 on weekdays
€130 on weekends
Length: Blue: 6,936 yards
White: 6,676 yards
Buggies and Trolleys: Both

Tee Times: Any day but Tuesday. Weekends are crowded.

County Louth Golf Club
Baltray, Drogheda
Co. Louth, Ireland
Tel. (353-41) 988-1530
Fax. 988-1531
reservations@countylouthgolfclub.com
www.countylouthgolfclub.com

The European Club

Founded in 1993
Brittas Bay, Co. Wicklow

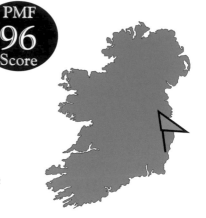

PMF 96 Score

- Ireland's best designer's ultimate creation…
- How much better is Tiger Woods than you? Here's how to find out…
- Why 20 holes are better than 18… and more

I n 1973 Pat Ruddy, who is easily the most important man in Irish golf today, bought some land near the County Sligo town of Ballymote. He wanted to build a golf course.

It was a disaster. The ground was wrong. He didn't have enough money. And people were stealing equipment. So Pat Ruddy cut his losses and walked away.

But in 1987, he got another chance.

Ruddy rented a helicopter and flew around the country looking at land suitable for a links course. He spotted an ad in the property section of a Dublin newspaper that detailed a stretch south of Dublin. The area is called Brittas Bay, between Arklow and Wicklow.

The ad said the land could possibly be used for a caravan park… or a golf course.

Ruddy knew right away he'd found the perfect piece of turf. Even better—it was the only piece of undeveloped land on the entire east coast of Ireland that was suitable for a proper links golf course.

The problem was, Ruddy didn't have any money. So he borrowed what he could to buy the land and did almost all of the construction work

Three Irish friends who joined me at The European Club: Derry (the pro at Faithlegg), Kevin, and Sean.

himself, with the help of friends and family.

Ruddy says today: "I can drive every machine." Along the way, Ruddy spent every spare penny he had on his project. He remortgaged his home. He sold his insurance policy and his car.

Look at the size of that sand dune! Everything about The European Club is dramatic and breathtaking.

Then, he got a break when the Irish tourism board, Bord Failte, began handing out grants for golf course projects. Even so, the course took five years to build. It finally opened in 1992.

Today, The European Club, despite the fact that it is less than two decades old, is the best links course in Ireland. Unlike most golf clubs in the country, which are owned by the members or a group of investors, The European Club is owned entirely by Pat Ruddy and his family.

I've played The European Club a half-dozen times in the past five years. In short, it's a truly spectacular place.

This course has some of the best dunes, best views, and best hole layouts in Ireland or anywhere else in the world. It's the kind of course that's worth traveling several hours to play—and it's hard to believe the course has been around for only 15 years. As Ruddy says: "What I'm trying to do at The European Club is accelerated evolution. To do what St. Andrews did in 400 years, what Royal Dublin and Portmarnock did in 100 years, and do it in fifteen." He's done it, no doubt.

The European Club is the kind of place where you eagerly await the next hole, to see what Ruddy has in store. It's one of the few courses in the world where you can play from the beach after an errant shot. Yes, you can ground your club. When I played here in mid October, it was in better shape than any other links course in the country.

I played with three Irish friends: Kevin, Sean, and Derry (who's the pro at Faithleg Golf Club in Waterford). We had a glorious day, if a bit rushed, as Kevin and his father-in-law-to-be had to hurry back to Tramore for a wedding rehearsal. I had to hurry off

Photo courtesy of The European Club

There can't be a course owner anywhere who tweaks his course as often as Pat Ruddy—on my recent trip he was talking about adding 30 bunkers.

too, to squeeze a late round in at Rosslare, more than 90 minutes south of The European Club. (Never miss the chance to attend an Irish wedding, by the way—it was one of the highlights of my trip.)

Pat Ruddy has said that one of his goals for The European Club is to keep the course as uncrowded as possible. We played at 8 am on a Thursday before a bank holiday weekend. We had the first time of the day—and there was not another till 2 pm. We didn't see another person on the course the whole time we were there. Amazing.

There are actually 20 holes at The European Club—you can play the two extras if you want. As Ruddy says in his "Philosophy" brochure that comes with your scorecard: "The links consists of two loops of 10-holes instead of two loops of 9-holes. This decimalised set-up is appropriate at a place called The European Club. Seriously, the real reason for this situation is this: If there are 20 fine golf holes out there, why stop at 18? We are here to play golf!"

As I write, Ruddy is making a tough course even tougher. He's adding 30 new bunkers for the Irish amateur championships that will be held there in the next year or so. "Bunkers are hazards," says Ruddy. They are not meant to be pleasure beaches. They are places of penance. Why have them if they do not punish?"

Pat Ruddy is a big bear of a man, but despite the fact that he owns Ireland's best golf course, and is in constant demand as a designer, he couldn't be more down-to-earth and unpretentious.

Only in Ireland would the country's top designer answer an unsolicited e-mail from an unknown travel writer (me). He even wrote a chapter for this book. I had nothing to offer but my thanks.

One final note: Want to find out how much better Tiger Woods is than you? Try playing The European Club from the back tees. Tiger shot a course-record 67 from the tips on his first visit in July of 2002. He was in town with David Duval, Scott McCarron, and Mark O'Meara, who were all on their way to the British Open at Muirfield. There are actually four sets of tees at The European Club. From the tips it's a very tough 7,300 yards. As Ruddy suggests: "Only players approaching championship standard off the blues."

One more thing: The only letdown at The European Club is the clubhouse, which does not serve beer or food. So the best place to go for a drink and a meal after your round at The European Club is Jack White's Pub, which you'll pass as you turn off the main N11 road towards the golf course.

This pub is one of the most famous in Ireland, and has been in this location for more than 200 years. In 1996, the place made national headlines when owner Tom Nevin was shot dead while counting the cash register after the St. Patrick's Day weekend. Tom's wife Catherine was convicted of mur-

Want to see just how good Tiger Woods is? Try playing The European Club from the tips (7,300 yards), where Tiger shot a 67.

der in a wildly publicized trial. She hired three men on various dates to murder her husband, before selling the place for €620,000 in 1998. Just to show you what's happened in Irish real estate during the past few years, the pub sold in 2003 for €2.5 million, and is undoubtedly worth much more now.

■ **What's good:** Best condition of any links course I played. The fairways are just incredible for links land. Elevated tee boxes on almost every hole—fairways often channel through high bunkers… railway sleepers ring every bunker and make for entertaining bounces… beautiful views of Mizen Head and the Irish Sea. No blind tee-shots… you always get to see where your ball is going. Pat Ruddy loves links golf more than anyone I've ever met—he's constantly out on the course, making small improvements to bunkers, dunes, tee boxes, etc. There's a max of 150 members, which means the course is never crowded. It has everything you want in a great links challenge—high dunes… big elevations, uneven fairways… scenic views of the sea and beach—you can even play your ball from the beach on #12. One of the best links courses in the world… 20 holes instead of 18, and these two "extras" are good enough to be included on even the best links courses. Play here in the off-season and it's half-price—probably the best golf bargain in the country.

■ **What's not:** The clubhouse is a big letdown. No bar, no decent food, and no views of the course. That's the only thing I hope Mr. Ruddy will change. Well… maybe I'd change #18 too. Many people complain about the man-made lake in front of the green. I don't mind that—it's just that the hole is

The European Club has lots of great holes, but the 12th is my favorite—The Irish Sea runs the length of the right side.

such a letdown of a finish after the other spectacular 19.

■ **Best hole:** *Golf Magazine* ranks three of The European Club's holes among the world's 500 best: the par-4 7th was in the top 100… and the par-5 13th and par-3 14th are ranked in the top 500. But for me, the best hole is number 12. It's a par-4, 459 yards from the blue tees… 438 yards from the whites. The entire hole runs along the beach, and from the highly elevated tee box, you have a spectacular view of the Irish Sea. The hole is fairly wide, so you can take a big swing… and when the wind is at your back you can probably hit the ball more than 300 yards, even if you've never done that before in your life. Then there's the green. At 127 yards, it's the longest green in the world (9 yards longer than the widest double-green at St. Andrews). Ever hit a 100-yard putt? You might here. One more thing I love about the 12th is that the beach is in play.

The European Club Details

PMF Score: 96

Design: 30 out of 30
Challenge: 29 out of 30
Condition: 20 out of 20
19th hole: 17 out of 20

Price: €150 every day of the week; November to March is half-price: €75

Length: Blue: 7,323 yards
White: 6,710 yards

Buggies and Trolleys: Trolleys, but no buggies or caddies.

Tee Times: You can play any day of the week, but must pay entire greens fee up-front on credit card. Cancellations incur a 10% charge. No refunds within 21 days of tee time.

The European Club

Brittas Bay
Co. Wicklow, Ireland
Tel. (353-404) 47415
Fax. 47449
e-mail: info@theeuropeanclub.com
www.theeuropeanclub.com

The Island Golf Club

Founded in 1890
Corballis, Co. Dublin

■ No golf on Sundays?…
■ The best course in the Dublin area…
■ The narrowest fairway you've ever seen…
and more

I n Ireland you can't play golf on Sundays.
At least that was the rule at most golf clubs in the late 1800s.
So on a warm September day in 1887, four members of the Royal Dublin Golf Club went on a mission to find a place to build their own golf course, where they could make their own rules.

The four Dubliners hopped in a rowboat and paddled across the body of water that separates the North Dublin village of Malahide from the spur of land to the north—known locally as "The Island."

What they found were 25-foot-high dunes covered in marram grass… tons of orchids and other flowers… and a land populated with wild and exotic birds: stonechats, skylarks and meadow pipits, to name a few.

In short, the men had stumbled upon prime golf terrain—probably the best links land within a 50-mile radius of Dublin's city center.

Ten men leased the land and founded The Island Golf Club in 1890.

They laid out the course between the high dunes without moving any soil… and for decades made the last part of the journey to the course by boat. It was the only way to get to The Island.

The 10 founders, known as "The Syndicate," sold annual memberships to outsiders beginning in 1896 (includ-

Although Portmarnock gets all the attention, The Island is the best links course in the Dublin area.

ing women a year later).

For the next five decades, the only way you got to play The Island was to be invited by a member. The original syndicate members kept their number at 10 until 1952, when they handed over interest in the club to the other members.

Today, The Island Golf Club is located on the same magnificent strip of land—it's a barrier island, much like the land where the more famous Portmarnock Golf Club is located.

But unlike Portmanock, the terrain around The Island is peppered with spectacular dunes, which lie in a series of north/south-oriented ridges. The golf course, for the most part, lies in the valleys of these ridges. It's a beautiful setting, with surrounding harbors, tidal inlets, and salt marshes.

This is, no doubt, a great links golf course—one of the 10 best in Ireland, and easily the best in Dublin.

The Island is full of unique and interesting holes—the super-narrow par-4 14th... the 13th over a waste area next to the coast... the long and winding par-5 15th, to name a few.

It's the kind of course where you can't wait to get to the next tee box to see what's in store—that's the sign of a really great course.

The Island has everything you want in a great links golf course: high dunes, deep bunkers, elevations, views of the sea (and the city, harbor and marina), and fast and true greens.

You can tell from the very beginning this is going to be a good golf course. Number 1 starts out great, with tremendous dunes on both sides of

With the beautiful scenery near The Island, it's hard to believe you're only a few miles from the city center.

the fairway. You won't be let down at any point in your round.

I spent some time talking to the pro, Kevin Kelliher. He's been at The Island for seven years, and is the first pro the club has ever had. This is a very welcoming but private and unpretentious place. The members want to keep their little slice of golf heaven a secret as long as possible.

Kelliher said the course is a bit short to host major tournaments, but the members are considering work that would add about 500 yards. But with tournaments comes notoriety—and lots of visitors—and many members would rather keep things just the way they are. I don't blame them—I would do the same.

■ **What's good:** This is a top-10 course, among the best in the country. It's easily the best in the Dublin area. If you are in Dublin, and have time for only one round, this should be it. Also: great condition… great history… friendly pro and members. Early-bird special during the week (before 8 am) is a great deal at €80. Remember: To most Irish early tee times are like dentist visits—something to avoid unless absolutely necessary.

■ **What's not:** Getting in and out of Dublin can be a traffic nightmare. If you're strictly going for golf, stay in the charming little nearby town of Malahide, rather than Dublin. It has everything you need—great bars, shops, restaurants, etc. And it puts you within a 20-minute drive of the area's best courses.

A look back from the first green towards the first tee and
clubhouse. It's easy to see why this is a top-10 course.

■ **Best hole:** The long and winding par-5 15th is a great hole… but my favorite is the super-short 345-yard par-4 14th that seems to play much shorter than this distance. This is a great risk/reward hole. It has the narrowest fairway I've ever seen—it can't be more than 25 yards

None of the other courses near Dublin have dunes as big as the ones you'll find on The Island's first hole.

across. Hit it straight and you're in great shape. Miss it and you're looking at bogey at best because you're not likely to find your ball.

The Island Details

PMF Score: 90
Design: 27 out of 30
Challenge: 27 out of 30
Condition: 18 out of 20
19th hole: 18 out of 20
Price: €125 all the time; early-bird rate (€85) on some weekdays.
Length: White: 6,826 yards
Green: 6,467 yards
Buggies and Trolleys: Both
Tee Times: Tee time restrictions

every day—see website. 50% deposit, refundable with at least two weeks notice.

The Island Golf Club
Corballis, Donabate,
Co. Dublin, Ireland
Tel. (353-1) 843-6205
Fax. 843-6860
louise@theislandgolfclub.com
www.theislandgolfclub.com

Laytown & Bettystown Golf Club

PMF
74
Score

Founded in 1909
Bettystown, Co. Meath

■ A four-hole golf course in your own backyard…
■ The home of Ireland's two most-famous golfers…
■ Ireland's next great course?… and more

H ave you ever dreamed of building a backyard golf course?
Not a full 18… but just a handful of nice holes you could play any
time of day, any day of the year. No tee times. No crowds. No slow
play. You'd not only have the perfect practice ground, but also the ultimate
backyard entertainment. I have this dream. And it's exactly what a fellow
named Tom Gilroy did about 100 years ago, near the little Irish coastal village of Bettystown, about 40 miles north of Dublin.

Gilroy was actually a Scotsman, who lived in nearby Coney Hall. He had a
4 handicap, and was considered Ireland's best player at the time.

Gilroy built his own four-hole layout. It was not open to the public but
rather intended only for Gilroy, his friends, and family. And Gilroy kept it that
way for several years, expanding bit by bit. Eventually, the course became too
much for him to handle on his own, so it was incorporated as Laytown &
Bettystown Golf Club in 1909 and expanded to a full 18 holes in 1913.

I've mentioned more than once in this book that it's becoming increasingly
hard to find the "undiscovered" in Ireland. Roughly 250,000 golfers visit the
Emerald Isle every year,
and the number of locals
who can now afford the
game increases daily.

But I was optimistic
on my trip. I knew I'd
still find a handful of
secrets—great golf
courses I'd never heard
or read about.

Laytown &

*I expected a mediocre links at best at Laytown, but it's a course that's
worth playing if you are anywhere nearby.*

170

Bettystown is one of those places.

It's a course I've never heard anyone say anything good about. In fact, the day before we arrived, a man working behind the front desk of the hotel where we stayed said Laytown "was not worth the trip."

I was expecting an unimaginative municipal course—like the tracts I'd found at Bundoran or Dunfanaghy.

But I was shocked at how nice a course Laytown is. The front nine is fantastic—played between high dunes and high rough, with great views of the Irish Sea. If the back nine was as good as the front, it could be a top-20 course.

That's the main problem with Laytown—the back nine is a huge letdown. Even so, the course is still worth your time, and still finishes in my top 30.

And, I have a two-part prediction.

About 25 miles southwest of Laytown lies the Tara mine—one of Europe's largest producers of zinc and lead. For the past few decades, prices for these commodities have gone nowhere.

But over the past few years, commodities like lead and zinc have been getting more and more expensive. I think it's a trend that will continue over the next decade. If so, there's going to be a lot more money in this area. And someone is going to put some serious cash into Laytown & Bettystown.

If you lengthened the course by about 1,000 yards, and redesigned the back nine, it could easily move up a dozen spots.

As you can see, the houses are right on top of the links course at Laytown—it needs about 1,000 extra yards and a back-nine makeover to be a really top links.

Laytown hosted a lot of the big Irish tournaments in the 1960s. Dunlop sponsored the Irish Open here in 1966. The winning prize was a whopping I£1,000. That's what a sorry state Irish golf was in during the 1950s and 1960s, before Americans and other foreigners discovered the Irish links.

One more interesting note: Laytown was the home of two of Ireland's most famous and successful golfers— Des Smith and Phillip Walton. Christy O'Connor, another of Ireland's most famous golfers, also played a lot of golf here.

■ **What's good:** Front nine is great—everything you'd expect from links golf, except that it's a little short, measuring not much more than 3,000 yards. This is truly a "hidden gem," as the Irish like to say. The terrain is more interesting than the links of the nearby (and much more popular) County Louth Golf Club. On the clubhouse wall, there's an interesting poster series of the history of Laytown.

■ **What's not:** The course is much too short to move up in the rankings... and the back nine is a big letdown. It's even too short for the better-than-average club player. From the tips it's only 6,448 yards, and there are only two par-5s. The back nine is disappointingly played inland, away from the coast and the big dunes.

■ **Best hole:** Number 7, a 397-yard par-4 in which you drive from an elevated tee with a nice view of the coast. It's a bit of a dogleg, and you have to hit around an odd little tree in the middle of the fairway—the only tree on the course as far as I could tell.

Laytown & Bettystown Details

PMF Score: 74
Design: 22 out of 30
Challenge: 21 out of 30
Condition: 15 out of 20
19th hole: 16 out of 20
Price: €60 Mon. – Friday
€75 Sat. – Sunday
Length: White: 6,448 yards
Green: 6,266 yards

Buggies and Trolleys: Trolleys only
Tee Times: No restrictions

Laytown & Bettystown Golf Club
Bettystown
Co. Meath, Ireland
Tel. (353-41) 982-7170
Fax. 982-8506
e-mail: links@landb.ie
website: www.landb.ie

Portmarnock Golf Club

Founded in 1894
Portmarnock, Co. Dublin

PMF
78
Score

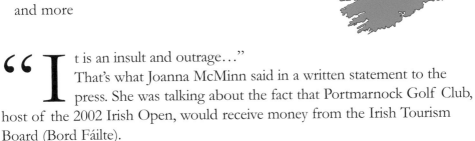

- No women allowed…
- The world's most expensive golf cart…
- Why you might need a note from your doctor…
  and more

"It is an insult and outrage…"
That's what Joanna McMinn said in a written statement to the press. She was talking about the fact that Portmarnock Golf Club, host of the 2002 Irish Open, would receive money from the Irish Tourism Board (Bord Fáilte).

Why was Ms. McMinn so upset?

Because women are not allowed to be members at Portmarnock. This rule has been in place since the club was founded in 1894. Women are allowed to play the course… they just can't be members. The club says that as a private organization it can make up its own membership policy. Sounds reasonable to me.

The government agency called the Equality Authority (no, I'm not making that up) decided to take Portmarnock to court, claiming the club is "discriminating," according to the country's Equal Status Act.

The stakes were high because if Portmarnock lost the case, their alcohol license could be suspended… indefinitely.

The case first went to the Dublin District Court… then the High Court.

When the ruling came down in favor of the Equality Authority, it sent shockwaves through the Portmarnock clubhouse.

Portmarnock is the most famous course in the East. It has hosted more big championships than any other course in the Republic.

Niall Crowley, chief executive of the Equality Authority, said the landmark ruling sent a clear message that banning women members was unacceptable. "This is the first time under the Equal Status Act that sanctions have been applied," he said.

The penalty? Portmarnock would lose its liquor license… *for seven whole days.* My source at the club told me they never closed for even a single day. And are women allowed to be members now? No, although they are allowed to play the course with a member.

What I don't understand is why women want to be members here so badly.

I guess like everything else in life, you want most what you can't have, whether it's actually worth having or not.

One thing for sure about Portmarnock… it has a great reputation.

If you read books and magazine articles about Irish links golf, you'll certainly hear great things about the place.

David Feherty, the joke-a-minute golf commentator from Northern Ireland, says this is "probably the best course in Ireland." (Feherty is a member here, by the way.) And he's not the only one singing Portmarnock's praises…

Golf Digest says this is the 40th-best course in the world… and the 4th-best in Ireland. *Golf Magazine* says it's the 3rd-best in Ireland.

To me, Portmarnock may be in the top three in Dublin—but it's nowhere near Ireland's overall top-10.

I've never seen a golf writer rank Portmarnock lower than the top-10 in Ireland. It's a great course, but it barely makes my top 25.

There's nothing particularly memorable... or unique. It's very flat, mostly uninteresting land. I think the place receives its high rankings by reputation alone.

When you read the glowing descriptions of Portmarnock in other publications, you'll get a feel for what I mean. Writers can never point to what, specifically, is so good about the place... so they resort to weak metaphors. Take, for example, the otherwise excellent book *Links of Heaven*, by Richard Phinney and Scott Whitley.

Here's their description of Portmarnock:

> "Like the Old Course at St. Andrews, Portmarnock invites metaphors, not photographs. It is a mood as much as a place, its charm an accumulated effect of the variety, intelligence and grace of the layout. There is a wonderful sense of proportion at Portmarnock, a feeling that every piece is in the perfect place. If Mozart had been a golf architect, this would have been his masterpiece."

Huh? Yes, Portmarnock is a good course. But it's not one of Ireland's best... and it's hard to justify the hefty €165 price tag.

What Portmarnock does have that few courses can match is an incredible history. In fact, there can be little debate about the fact that this is Ireland's most important golf course over the last 50 years. (Portrush, however, could put up a good argument.)

At the beginning of the twentieth century, this was certainly *the* club to belong to in Ireland. And as *Barron's* said recently, for many this is still the case.

The course hosted Ireland's biggest tournament (the Irish Open) a dozen times in the 1970s and 80s. Phil Mickelson helped the U.S. win the Walker Cup (the Ryder Cup for amateurs) here in 1991.

Portmarnock actually has three nine-hole courses. The red course is the

World's Most Expensive Golf Cart

Joe Carr was asked to play a round of golf with U.S. President Dwight D. Eisenhower at Portmarnock Golf Club.

Carr was one of Ireland's best amateur golfers of the past 100 years, and represented the country 10 times in the Walker Cup (the Ryder Cup for amateurs).

The only condition to the round was that the club supply Eisenhower with a golf cart, because of his heart condition. This was long before Americans were traveling to Ireland for golf vacations. And as Joe Carr put it, "there wasn't a single golf cart in all of Ireland."

So in order to get the U.S. President to come to Portmarnock, the club arranged for an open-top Rolls Royce to be used instead, and the round went off without a hitch.

front nine and the blue is the back nine of the "championship" course. The yellow nine is a slightly shorter layout that looks, from quick glances at just a few holes, like it is probably as good as or better than the more famous nines.

The day we played Portmarnock was grand opening night for the new clubhouse. At the guarded entrance, we had to wait a few extra minutes while the security guard radioed the clubhouse. The course, you see, was closed to visitors. Somehow the message had not gotten from my contact, Secretary John Quigley, to the guard, that we were arriving late in the afternoon for a quick round. This was a minor inconvenience, however, and it proves just how open Irish courses are to the golfing public and to visitors.

Imagine trying to get onto a private U.S. course on a big day like this, when most of the members would be showing up in jacket and tie for a gala dinner. In the U.S. you'd never be allowed up the driveway, much less onto the course. But in Ireland, it's a different story.

■ **What's good:** The history—Portmarnock sits on ground that was once owned by the Jameson family (of whiskey fame) and the club's flagpole came from a Jameson family yacht. The tradition: You need a note from your doctor to get a golf cart. The first tee box is spectacular. It's the biggest tee box I've ever seen, at

This is hallowed golfing ground—all of Europe's great players have visited Portmarnock. The course is built on land once owned by the Jameson family, of whiskey fame.

least 50 yards long, and perfectly manicured, right next to the pro shop and the caddie-hire station. You don't have to be perfect with your tee shots here—it's a good course for the high handicapper who wants a true links experience. The bunkers are spectacular—deep and in perfect condition.

At €190 per round on weekends this is one of the most overpriced courses in the country.

■ **What's not:** Mostly an uninteresting design… few unique and memorable holes… played out mostly over flat and uninspiring land. Could be the most over-priced golf course in the country. Reputation and history are better than the golf.

■ **Best hole:** #14 is probably the best hole—it seems like a pretty easy par-4… till you see the three big bunkers in front of the hard-to-hit green. #12 is good too—an uphill par-3. And #15 is a tough par-3 along the coast—the club's most famous hole. It's nice to see the water after playing inland for so long.

Portmarnock Details

PMF Score: 78
Design: 20 out of 30
Challenge: 22 out of 30
Condition: 18 out of 20
19th hole: 18 out of 20 (I wasn't allowed in the new clubhouse, but it looks nice from the outside.)
Price: €165 on weekdays
        €190 on weekends
Length Blue tees: 7,365 yards;
White: 6,900; Green: 6,684.
(9-hole Yellow course): Blue tees: 3,461; White: 3,357
Buggies and Trolleys: Trolleys and caddies. Buggies, with medical note.

Tee Times: Every day but Wednesday and Saturday mornings, but there are restrictions to times. You must pay up-front with credit card. 50% is non-refundable.

Portmarnock Golf Club
Portmarnock
Co. Dublin, Ireland
Tel. (353-1) 846-2634
Fax. 846-2602
clare@portmarnockgolfclub.ie
www.portmarnockgolfclub.ie

Portmarnock Hotel & Golf Links

Founded in 1997
Portmarnock, Co. Dublin

PMF
66
Score

■ Bernhard Langer's shot at links design…
■ The friendliest starter in Ireland…
■ The whiskey family's golf course… and more

W e were late. Really late.

We had a mid-morning tee time at Portmarnock Hotel & Golf Links, and pulled into the parking lot about one minute before we were scheduled to be on the tee. We grabbed our shoes and clubs and literally ran to the pro shop. Now it was already after our scheduled time.

It was a warm Saturday morning in mid-October. A perfect day for golf, and the course, located just 20 minutes from Dublin, was packed. Cars were parked on the grassy area next to the lot. If we didn't make our time I knew we would at the very least get a scolding from the pro shop and the starter… and might miss our round altogether.

Playing two courses in a day made it impossible to adjust our schedule by even a few hours. That's what happens when you try to cover 44 courses in a month.

In the pro shop, several people were lined up in front of us. Now, it was a good 10 minutes after our scheduled time. Our chances of playing were getting slimmer by the minute.

We explained to the guys in the pro shop how we got lost. We apologized… and asked if there was any way we could play right

How easy-going are the Irish? We arrived 10 minutes late (on a packed day) for a time at Portmarnock H&G, and they let us off without a hitch.

178

away. They said they weren't sure, and sent us down to see the starter.

Now, in the United States, you have to be a "grumpy old white man" to be a golf course starter. Like the women who work behind the counter of every motor vehicle administration, these fellows revel in punishing you for not following the rules exactly.

Things looked even worse when we made our way to the first tee. A group of golfers were taking warm-up swings near the tee box... and at least a dozen other golfers were milling around nearby. We decided to take a chance, and approached the starter, expecting the worst.

He was a white-haired Irishman in his mid-60s, with a deep Irish brogue. With all of the anti-American sentiment in Ireland at the time, I figured this was all they needed—two "ugly" Americans showing up late for their tee time, still expecting to play.

But then... as soon as the starter began speaking, I remembered... *this is Ireland.*

First he said: "Slow down fellows... 'tis a lovely day." Then, surprisingly: "No worries, I'll get ye out in front of de groups warming up."

Then he calmly pulled us aside and explained the layout of the course... the markings... the history... and what we could expect. In short, this man couldn't have been nicer.

Bernhard Langer's design in Ireland could use a makeover, especially on the front nine.

Okay… so this was the nicest starter I've ever met. But surely, the guys waiting to play would be furious. We were forcing them to wait at least another 15 minutes before starting their round. "No problem," they told us. "It's a beautiful day. Go on ahead and enjoy the round." Wow.

Dublin's Trinity College, founded in 1592. It's the oldest college in the country, and home of the famous Book of Kells.

It's moments like these when you remember that golf in Ireland is great not just because of the links golf, but also because of the Irish charm. The folks at Portmarnock Hotel & Golf Links won us over on that October Saturday.

I just wish I had better things to report about the golf course, which opened for play in 1997, and was designed by Germany's best golfer, Bernhard Langer.

It's a good thing Bernhard was a great golfer… he would have had a hard time making a living as a designer. This was his first attempt in Ireland I'm told. It's not bad… but it's not very good either.

This is a fourth-tier course that might be worth playing if you are staying at the hotel or if you are in the area for a considerable amount of time. But unfortunately, it's not worth going out of your way to play.

This land does have an interesting history. It was originally owned by the Jameson family (of Irish whiskey fame and fortune). They had a nine-hole course on this land that is now part of both this course and the nearby Portmarnock Golf Club.

■ **What's good:** Starter was super-friendly… as was everyone else at the course. The guy who works in the men's locker room can tell you anything about any nearby golf course—he even has photocopied directions he'll be happy to share. People on the course let us play through three different times. It's easy and pretty straightforward. You can have an off day here and still score well. Like Ballybunion Old, there's a gravestone on the right of the first fairway. I read that St. Marnock is buried here.

- **What's not:** There are no real awe-inspiring holes… the course was not in very good condition… it was slow going, one of longest rounds of our entire trip… mostly flat and uninteresting land behind the dunes that guard the water. No view of the course from the bar or restaurant.
- **Best hole:** #16 is a 396-yard dogleg par-4. You tee off near the dunes and the beach, and then make a fairly sharp turn to the right, with dunes and high grass all around. If the rest of the course were like this it would rank much higher.

Portmarnock Hotel & Golf Details

PMF Score: 66

Design: 18 out of 30
Challenge: 18 out of 30
Condition: 14 out of 20
19th hole: 16 out of 20
Price: €125 weekdays and weekends
   high season
Length: Blue: 6,880 yards
   White: 6,591 yards
   Green: 6,204 yards

Buggies and Trolleys: Both
Tee Times: No restricted days. €4 on-line booking fee.

Portmarnock Hotel & Golf Links

Portmarnock
Co. Dublin, Ireland
Tel. (353-1) 846-0611
Fax. 846-2442
golfres@portmarnock.com
www.portmarnock.com

Rosslare Golf Club

Founded in 1905
Rosslare Strand, Co. Wexford

PMF
66
Score

- A clubhouse washed into the sea...
- The warmest and driest place in Ireland...
- Four rounds in one day for I£5... and more

O n December 16th, 1989, a terrible storm hit the southeast coast of Ireland.

The surging sea made its way inland, covering as much as 100 yards of Rosslare Golf Club. The sea flooded low-lying areas and eroded beaches, cliffs, and sand dunes. Bulkheads fell apart... roads and even houses were in danger of being completely washed away.

This is the plight of a links golf course. They are located next to the sea, and the sea never stops. It occasionally takes away big chunks of a great golf course that has stood for hundreds of years.

At Rosslare, the dunes have historically eroded at a rate of about two feet per year. And in a bad storm, like the one in December of 1989, a links course can lose 10 feet or more in a 24-hour period.

Over the past 100 years, Rosslare has lost the site of the original pavilion and several entire fairways. This means the course has to move progressively inland. Now there's plenty of money in Ireland to stop such erosion—but for almost the entire twentieth century, golf courses could do nothing but pray every winter that they'd be spared severe storm damage.

For courses like Rosslare, where there's not

In a bad storm a links course can lose as much as 10 feet of shoreline—that's what happened at Rosslare in a bad December storm in 1989.

a whole lot of land to start with, it means fairways, tee boxes, and greens are now a lot closer together than they used to be.

The folks here have done a good job, however, stretching this course out with the available land. Rosslare is plenty long for the average player—6,786 yards from the blue tees.

I have a special place in my heart for this golf course. When I spent a year living in Waterford, this was the closest links course to my home. I made the 45-minute drive about a dozen times.

> ## Four Rounds in One Day for I£5
>
> I thought I was doing pretty well walking two rounds in a day, but Tom Williams reports in his book about Rosslare that three members doubled my efforts in 1963...
>
> That year, a man named Tommy Hynes bet three members I£5 they couldn't each play four full rounds in one day at 75 or better, including handicaps. No buggies allowed. One break for lunch.
>
> A huge crowd turned out to watch—and bet— on the outcome. Most bet the men couldn't do it. Hynes banked on bad weather, but it was a glorious day. On the last hole of the last round, Edmund Wheeler (with a 16-handicap), needed a par for the three men to win the bet. He drove it in the fairway bunker, and the crowd gasped, believing they were about to win. But Wheeler hit a great 5-iron from the bunker, then a good approach, and putted out for both the par and the win.

Still, this is not a top-tier links course… or even a second or third-tier course. Instead it's a nice introduction to links golf—a great place to spend an enjoyable afternoon, where you can have a decent round without your best game. It's a relatively flat course, with little in the way of high grass.

You have to really hit a bad tee shot to lose it here.

Rosslare gets a lot of play because it's the only links course for miles around… and it's right next to the ferry that brings

Rosslare is the perfect course to play if you are taking the nearby to France or England.

British and French tourists on holiday.

This is another one of those courses that just barely managed to make it through Ireland's lean years. In Tom Williams' book *Fairways of the Sea*, he reports that in 1957 there were only about 50 active club members.

■ **What's good:** A good introduction to links golf, without many difficult challenges. Views of the beach and sea are nice… undulating fairways…

Rosslare barely survived Ireland's economic woes—in 1957 there were just 50 active members.

friendly welcome… and decent price. The soil drains quickly here. You can play this course even after a big storm. Because it's the driest and warmest part of the country, it's a great course to play in the winter.

- **What's not:** Very flat… course is squeezed onto a small piece of land. Several times you have to cross a fairway or hit a tee shot near a different green. No real memorable or stunning holes.

- **Best hole:** #7 is a tough 554-yard par-5 that runs entirely along the coast. It's always been my favorite. You can reach it in two with a strong breeze behind you… and will require four or more with a stiff breeze in your face.

Rosslare Details

PMF Score: 66
Design: 17 out of 30
Challenge: 16 out of 30
Condition: 16 out of 20
19th hole: 17 out of 20
Price: €40 on weekdays
   €60 on weekends
Length: Blue: 6,786; White: 6,597
Buggies and Trolleys: Both

Tee Times: No deposits and no restrictions, but Tuesdays and weekends are crowded.

Rosslare Golf Club
Rosslare Strand
Co. Wexford, Ireland
Tel. (353-53) 32203
Fax. 32263
e-mail: office@rosslaregolf.com
www.rosslaregolf.com

Royal Dublin Golf Club

Founded in 1885
Dollymount, Co. Dublin

PMF
65
Score

- Captain Bligh's golf course...
- Where Seve and Bernhard won Irish Opens...
- The man who turned down the Masters 20
  straight times... and more

C aptain William Bligh was asleep in his quarters.
In the middle of the night, members of his own crew stormed
Bligh's room, tied the Captain up, and marched him (along with 18
other officers) onto the ship's deck.

There the men were stuffed into a 23-foot launch boat... and shoved
into the sea to die.

But Bligh was an excellent sailor. He skippered the small vessel for 47
days and 3,618 nautical miles, landing in Timor, Java. Incredibly, everyone
survived.

That was in April, 1789. And this true story would become the subject
of both a book and several movies called *The Mutiny on the Bounty*.

What most people don't know about Captain Bligh is that he was also
instrumental in forming two of Ireland's links golf courses.

You see, about 100 years after Captain Bligh's adventure, a Scottish
banker named Lumsden set out a golf course in Dublin's Phoenix Park. The
park today is about 1,700 acres (twice as big as New York's Central Park),
located two miles west of the city center.

To construct his temporary golf course, Lumsden used glass jars and flags.

Like most of Ireland, Phoenix Park was consistently dry enough for
golf only in the summer. Fall, winter, and spring were simply too wet.

So Lumsden persuaded Dubliners to move the course. They found the
perfect spot on Bull Island.

It's a man-made stretch of land Captain Bligh helped create in the
Dublin Harbor. Bligh was instrumental in dredging the harbor to create a
shipping lane. Bull Island was a byproduct of the dredging. Like all good
Irish links courses, its sandy soil is perfect for year-round golf.

This golf course became the site of Royal Dublin—one of Ireland's most important links courses. (St. Anne's Golf Club is on the same piece of land.)

You might also see Royal Dublin called Dollymount—the name of the nearby neighborhood.

In the early 1900s, this was one of THE most exclusive and elite clubs in the entire country. The membership ranks were made up of lawyers, doctors, and other members of high society.

Royal Dublin was once the home of the country's biggest tournaments. When golf became popular in Ireland again in the 1960s, Royal Dublin hosted Irish Opens won by Bernhard Langer and Seve Ballesteros. Photos of Jack Nicklaus, Ballesteros, Langer, and other famous pros from the 1980s line the locker room walls.

Unfortunately, Royal Dublin's best days are behind it.

When I played Royal Dublin in November of 2004, the course was undergoing major renovations. Twelve of the 18 holes were finished but six were still under construction. Even with the major renovations, the main problem with Royal Dublin is that the terrain is almost entirely flat. It's missing the giant dunes and dramatic land of Ireland's best links.

Still, this course has great history, tradition, and a fantastic clubhouse. But the golf at Royal Dublin is at best mediocre. It's a flat and rather unimaginative layout. And it's hard to justify the price (€120).

In the early 1900s, Royal Dublin and Portmarnock were the most exclusive clubs in the Republic.

Perhaps the six new holes will make a big difference, but I doubt it.

This course needs a serious Pat Ruddy-like makeover. Unfortunately, I think Royal Dublin will continue to lurk in my fourth tier of Ireland's links rankings until they make some major changes.

One interesting note: Ireland's most popular golfer of all time, Christy O'Connor, was the pro at Royal Dublin for many, many years.

Known in Ireland simply as "Himself," O'Connor played on 10 Ryder Cup teams, won 32 events, finished second in the 1965 British Open, and won 9 Irish Open titles.

But my favorite anecdote about O'Connor is that he turned down an invitation to play in the Masters at Augusta National—*for 20 straight years*, from 1955 to 1974. "Golf was a different cup of tea than it is now, money-wise," O'Connor told *Golf Magazine* in April 2005, shortly after his 80th birthday. "I never had any sponsors, so who was going to pay my way to the States? I couldn't afford to—money wasn't that plentiful." O'Connor's top priority was his job as a club pro. He had six kids and a wife to feed at home.

■ **What's good:** I like that Royal Dublin has clung to its men-only status. Women can play, they just can't become members. The secretary told me "historically and traditionally it's been a men's course." The place does have great history (the British military used the course as a rifle range in World War II) and a very

Royal Dublin has hosted many of Ireland's most important tournaments, including several Irish Opens.

nice clubhouse (outdoor seating overlooks the links). There's a great pro shop and you'll get a very friendly welcome here. It's a true links course set on an island just outside of Dublin City center. Bull Island is filled with exotic birds and flowers. On any Saturday, you'll find Dubliners bird-watching with telescopes, and families strolling the roads and nearly paths. Nice views of the surrounding water and the city in the distance. It's hard to believe you're only a 20-minute drive (without traffic) to the city center.

■ **What's not:** The layout and design are uninspiring. No use of the surrounding water… little use of the dunes. Too expensive. Another candidate for "most over-priced course in the country." Doubtful the last six holes to be renovated can improve the course much.

■ **Best hole:** #18, called The Garden, is the most famous and probably the best hole on the course. It's a very flat but tough 442-yard par-4. It has a 90-degree dogleg with a stream that runs up the entire right side of the fairway, all the way to the green, finishing near the clubhouse. It's a great last hole that lets you make up, or lose, several strokes in a close match.

Royal Dublin Details

PMF Score: 65
Design: 16 out of 30
Challenge: 16 out of 30
Condition: 14 out of 20
19th hole: 19 out of 20
Price: €150 Mon.-Fri.
    €170 weekends
Length: 6,309 from blue tees
Buggies and Trolleys: Both

Tee Times: No visitors on Wednesdays or Saturdays, and limited times other days.

Royal Dublin Golf Club
Dollymount
Dublin 3, Ireland
Tel. (353-1) 833-6346
Fax. 833-6504
info@theroyaldublingolfclub.com
www.theroyaldublingolfclub.com

St. Anne's Golf Club

Founded in 1921
Dollymount, Co. Dublin

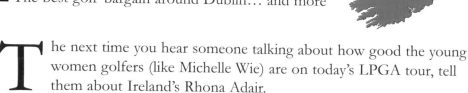

PMF
72
Score

- A 78-year-old pro versus a 17-year old Irish teenager…
- Where to find herons, oystercatchers, kestrels
- The best golf bargain around Dublin… and more

The next time you hear someone talking about how good the young women golfers (like Michelle Wie) are on today's LPGA tour, tell them about Ireland's Rhona Adair.

Rhona won the Women's British Open twice—once at the age of 18, and again a few years later.

And in July of 1899, she played a challenge match against one of the best golfers of the nineteenth century—Tom Morris (who won the British Open four times between 1860 and 1867).

At the time, Rhona was just 17 years old. Tom Morris was certainly well past his prime (at age 78), but like most men, he wasn't going to back down to a challenge from a woman… especially an Irish teenager.

Rhona Adair grew up playing Royal Portrush in Northern Ireland (when all of Ireland was still under British rule). Tom Morris, of course, spent most of his time at St. Andrews. He got his start there as a club maker, left for a brief stint at Prestwick, and returned to St. Andrews in 1865 first as greenskeeper and then head pro. He was affiliated

St. Anne's gets very little attention, but it's the third-best course in Dublin, after The Island and Portmarnock.

with the club for the next 43 years, until his death in 1908.

So the match was set. Old man Morris against upstart teenager Adair. The pair played a 36-hole, one-day contest at St. Andrews in Scotland.

Morris led by one after the first 18 holes. He stretched the lead to three after 27 holes. But with just nine to play, Adair began a late charge. She closed to within one. Morris won by a single stroke.

One thing you'll notice about women golfers in Ireland is that they are serious about the sport. And much tougher than most Americans (men and women) who play the game.

While playing Dingle Golf Club on a terribly rainy day, for example, I met two Dublin women, one of whom was in her 70s, the other in her 50s. They traveled all the way from the capital for a golfing weekend. It's at least a four-hour drive.

I was reminded of the story of Rhona Adair when I arrived at St. Anne's Golf Club outside of Dublin on a Saturday afternoon in November.

You see, I couldn't play the course because it was ladies competition day. So I walked the course instead, and talked with a handful of members.

St. Anne's is a nice, and overlooked, course. It's nearly as good as Portmarnock, and it's definitely better than Royal Dublin. It's by no means one of the best links in the country, but it's a decent third-tier course.

The links is actually located on the same piece of land (North Bull

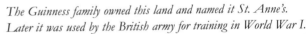

The Guinness family owned this land and named it St. Anne's. Later it was used by the British army for training in World War I.

Island) as Royal Dublin. And like Royal Dublin, the terrain is mostly flat. But at St. Anne's, the dunes are taller and more pronounced.

Located on Bull Island, a national wildlife preserve, St. Anne's is home to many exotic birds and plants.

- **What's good:** The history: The Guinness family owned this land and named it St. Anne's in 1837. In 1914 it was commandeered by the British Army as training grounds during World War I. The entire North Bull Island is a National Nature Preserve. You'll find herons, oystercatchers, kestrels, skylarks, brent geese, and all kinds of other exotic wildlife. Michael Collins (the famous Irish revolutionary) was active in the club for about 60 years. This is a good true links course… a mid-range challenge that is not at all overwhelming and should be playable even on a blustery day. It's almost as good as Portmarnock, and better than Royal Dublin—at a fraction of the price.

- **What's not:** The only real knock against St. Anne's is that it's so flat, but that does make it good for walking. Also, no elevation changes, or dramatic views… and no pro shop.

- **Best hole:** I met three single-digit-handicap members who said #1 was their favorite hole. But I liked #s 11 and 12, which have valley-like fairways, surrounded by tall dunes on both sides.

St. Anne's Details

PMF Score: 72
Design: 20 out of 30
Challenge: 17 out of 30
Condition: 17 out of 20
19th Hole: 18 out of 20
Price: €65 on weekdays
€75 on weekends
Length: Blue: 6,626 yards; White: 6,443; Yellow: 6,202
Buggies and Trolleys: Both
Tee Times: No deposit required.

Only weekend tee times for visitors are 10 am to 11 am on Saturday.

St. Anne's Golf Club
Bull Island Nature Reserve
Dollymount, Dublin 5, Ireland
Tel. (353-1) 833-6471
Fax. 833-4618
e-mail: info@stanneslinksgolf.com
www.stanneslinksgolf.com

8

Two Things (Besides Golf) You Should Try To Do While in Ireland

#1. Go to the races

In the United States, horseracing is a strange sport. The people you find at American racetracks typically fall into one of two groups.

First you have the people in the business—the owners, trainers, breeders, etc. Then there are the bettors—mostly middle-class folks wasting money that should be going towards the mortgage or utility bills.

But in Ireland, horseracing is a different kind of activity. For one, racetracks typically hold only a few events each year. So when the horses are running in Ireland, you can usually expect a big crowd. And it's usually a family event. You'll find women, kids, teenagers… even grandparents, especially on weekends. There's often live music. Everyone's drinking beers… placing small wagers, and generally having a grand old time. You can actually meet girls at the races in Ireland. You wouldn't dream of doing that in the States.

What really makes Irish horseracing great, however, are the bookies.

As you probably know, the only way to bet at the track in the United Sates is to place a wager with the track. But in Ireland, there are also at least a dozen bookies at every race. They set up temporary stands next to the clubhouse, typically with just a blackboard, a

At the racetrack in Ireland, you can make your bet with the track… or with one of the bookies who set up shop on the apron.

change purse, and an assistant. They use binoculars to check other bookies' odds. Assistants erase and rewrite furiously to keep prices competitive. Shop around for the best odds on your horse.

The best horseraces in Ireland are held in Galway every September. But it gets very crowded. This is one of the most popular social events of the year. Unless you want to make a whole trip of it, you're better off finding a track in a smaller town, where they are holding a several-day meet. For details, check out the Association of Irish Racetracks: www.air.ie.

The "fixtures" link shows you where the horses are running and when. The "racecourses" link shows you where the tracks are located. You'll find racecourses near several great links golf courses: Tralee, Sligo, Royal County Down, and Laytown, just to name a few.

Although many of the tracks have short meets, the country has more than 300 days of live racing every year—so there's almost always a race going on somewhere.

The horse business in general is booming in Ireland. The country also has about 40% of Europe's thoroughbred stud industry, largely because of tax incentives that give stud-farm owners full exemptions on both income and corporate taxes.

#2. Go to a hurling or Gaelic football match

Ireland has two national sports, both of which are played nowhere else in the world on a serious level. And the Irish are crazy for both of these games.

Hurling and Gaelic football are played on the same field, with the same goalposts and scoring system.

Gaelic football looks like a combination of basketball, soccer, and rugby. The ball is round. You can dribble and kick it. You score one point for hitting it through the American-

Photo: Mary Pat Fannon

Hurling is like field hockey on steroids—and played in the air. There are no professionals—even the top players have day jobs.

football-like uprights, and three points for scoring a goal (about the size of a soccer goal).

Gaelic football is good… but hurling is a much better sport to watch. It's played with what look like field hockey sticks (called "hurleys") and a hard ball that feels like a field hockey ball (called a "sliothar").

But unlike field hockey, hurling is played through the air.

You can balance or bounce the ball on your stick while you run, but you can't run with the sliothar in your hand for more than four steps. The objective is the same as Gaelic football—hit it through the uprights, or score in the goal.

Hurling is fast and violent. No gloves… no pads—but most players do wear helmets.

The great thing about both Irish games is that the players (even the best in the country) are amateurs. They all have day jobs and play for their local club teams. No contracts. No free agents. No trades. You play for your hometown for life.

Photo: Mary Pat Fenton

Hurling matches go on almost all year round. The All-Ireland Championships take place in Dublin each fall.

Local club matches take place throughout the year. Then, the best players represent their county (remember there are 26 counties in the Republic, and 6 in the North) compete for the All-Ireland Championship. The finals are held at Dublin's famous Crooke Park each fall.

Hurling has been around in some form for more than 3,000 years. Counties Galway, Kilkenny, and Tipperary dominate the sport, and have won two-thirds of the championships since the current system started in 1884.

For a schedule of matches, go to www.gaa.ie, and click on the "fixtures" link. Or just ask in any pub in any town when the next Gaelic football or hurling match will be played. You can bet on the match before you go at one of the bookmaker shops found in every city and in every small town.

9

Recommended Golf Trips

P art of the fun of taking a golf trip to Ireland is making the plans. Get your friends together, add a bunch of Guinness, and let the discussions begin. I recommend you hire a driver no matter which trip you take. In fact, if you have to save money, and need to choose between luxury accommodations and a chauffeur, the choice is easy. Here are a few of my recommended trips:

● The ultimate, best of Ireland golf adventure: two weeks

This is a no-expenses-spared journey. You'll get all 10 of the best links

courses in Ireland. Do not try to drive it, however. Instead, fly into Shannon, and helicopter to Old Head. Next helicopter to Waterville, and then drive to the other great courses of the southwest: Tralee, Ballybunion (Old Course), and Lahinch. Helicopter to the

The beach on the Irish Sea side of The European Club's coastal holes is in play. Yes, you can ground your club without penalty.

Northwest to play at least two of the following: Portsalon, Rosapenna, and Enniscrone. Helicopter to the North to play either Portstewart or Portrush.

Next drive to Royal County Down, then helicopter to The European Club south of Dublin. Spend the night in Dublin and play The Island before flying home from Dublin. Eleven rounds of golf in 14 days.

● Introduction to Ireland's great links #1: Nine days in the Southwest

This is where most golfers go on their first trip to Ireland. As much as I'd like to tell you to do something different, it's hard to argue with a region that has four of the country's top five courses.

Fly into Shannon Airport. Be sure to play Lahinch, Tralee, Waterville, Old Head, and Ballybunion (Old or Cashen). If you want to squeeze in another round, make it Dooks or Doonbeg. If you want to cut out a lot of driving time, cut Old Head, or consider getting a helicopter for the day.

A nine-day trip means you can leave the United States on a Friday night, arrive Saturday morning in Ireland, and play golf every day but one. Fly home the following Sunday, also out of Shannon.

● Introduction to Ireland's great links #2: nine days in the North/Northwest

Here's another great introductory trip that combines courses in the North and the Northwest. You get 4 of the top 11 courses… and 5 of the top 15.

Leave the U.S. Friday night and fly into Shannon with a connecting flight to Derry if possible. If not, prepare for a long drive, and don't schedule a round of golf that day until late afternoon.

This trip has the best concentration of good links courses, with the least amount of between-course driving. Don't miss Portsalon, Rosapenna (Sandy Hills), Ballyliffin, Portstewart, and Portrush (Dunluce). All of these courses are among the 15 best in the country.

If you want more golf play the new Ruddy-Morris

A great first trip to Ireland is the North-Northwest combo. You get five of the top 15 courses. Pictured here: Portstewart.

links at Rosapenna, the Valley Links at Portrush, then Castlerock, in that order. And remember, nearby St. Patrick's is now being redesigned by Jack Nicklaus, and could be a top-10 course in two years. I like this trip, because it gives you a taste of both Northern Ireland and the Republic. And you get to play a handful of great links courses most Americans have never heard of.

● Ireland's best bargain golf trip: Nine days in the Northwest

You might consider making the Northwest your first trip if you want to 1) save money or 2) play courses that are less crowded and less touristy. Golf in the northwest region costs, on average, about one-third less than what you'll pay in every other region. Accommodations are also about 25% cheaper.

In this region, don't miss Portsalon, Enniscrone, and Rosapenna (Sandy Hills)— the three best in the Northwest. I also recommend you try the Ruddy-Morris Links at Rosapenna. I haven't played the new back nine designed by Pat Ruddy, but I doubt Pat Ruddy will disappoint. Keep in mind: Rosapenna is a very nice

The best golf deals in Ireland are in the Northwest, where it costs about 30% less than elsewhere. Pictured here: Sligo.

(and inexpensive) hotel and resort. Stay here and it's easy to reach Portsalon and St. Patrick's too. And remember, St. Patrick's, which is literally right next door to Rosapenna, is now being redesigned by Jack Nicklaus. In a year or two, it's likely this region will have the best four or five courses in the country within one 25-mile radius.

The other courses worth playing in this region are Ballyliffin (play Glashedy then Old Links), Carne, Donegal, and Sligo, in that order. Leave the U.S. Friday night and fly into Shannon. Hire a driver or rent a car and head northwest to Enniscrone. To avoid the long drive after arriving in Ireland, look into a connecting flight to Knock or Sligo airports.

● Your Third Trip to Ireland: Nine Days in the North

After you've played the southwest and the northwest Irish links courses, try Northern Ireland. There are four great links courses here: Portstewart, Portrush (both courses) and Royal County Down.

If you want more golf, Ardglass should be your next choice, followed by Castlerock. When you land in either Shannon or Dublin, get a connecting flight to Derry or Belfast, where you can rent a car or hire a driver.

● A golf trip with the wife and kids: Nine days in the East

There are several good reasons to take a golf trip to eastern Ireland. For one, it's a good trip if you've got people joining you who don't play golf.

Remember, most of the links courses in Ireland are located in very small towns, where there's little to do besides golf. Dublin, on the other hand, has tons of great tourist attractions: historic churches and buildings, great shopping, centuries-old pubs and restaurants,

The nice thing about a trip to Dublin is that there's plenty to do for those who aren't playing golf. Pictured here: O'Connell St. Bridge.

great theater and music, brewery tours, etc.

If you take a golf trip to the East, the two must-plays are The Island and The European Club. For more golf, play Portmarnock Golf Club, St. Anne's, County Louth, and Laytown & Bettystown, in that order. Fly in and out of Dublin.

All of the links courses near Dublin are northeast of the city, so if you're going for golf only, avoid Dublin traffic by staying in the charming town of Malahide.

● How to have a great golf vacation by staying put

If you want a vacation where you can unpack your bags just once, and still play a handful of great links golf courses, my #1 choice is the resort and golf courses at Rosapenna. It's understated, elegant, and downright cheap.

You can stay here for a week and play a handful of great links golf courses. The Sandy Hills and Morris-Ruddy links at Rosapenna are at your doorstep. Portsalon, another top-10 course, is 30 minutes away. And St. Patrick's, now being redesigned by Jack Nicklaus, is right next door.

This is a 4-star resort with a spa, a nice bar, a snooker table, a very good restaurant, and a pool. Frank Casey and his staff will arrange horse rides and fishing expeditions. Best of all, the place is a screaming bargain—less than €100 per night any time of the year, and that includes breakfast. The downside is that Rosapenna is in the middle of nowhere—Belfast (3 hours away) is the nearest international airport.

Here are several other places you might consider for a stay-in-one-place vacation. I haven't stayed at any of these places personally. Some were recommended to me—others I found in my readings.

Southwest:

The Dubliner ranks The Admiralty Lodge one of Ireland's 50 best hotels. It's a 4-star guesthouse close to a 9-hole links course called Spanish Point, and not far from the great courses at Doonbeg and Lahinch. Price: €115 to €165 a night. www.admiralty.ie

A wealthy friend who owns real estate all over the world and has traveled to more than 150 countries swears by the Sheen Falls Lodge—one of the most luxurious resorts in the country. Waterville, Tralee, and Dooks are within a 60-mile radius. Killarney, one of the best inland courses in the country, is 20 miles away. Rates in the high season are €400 to €1,800 a night. www.sheenfallslodge.ie.

You can be closer to the great southwest links by staying in Killarney. One good choice is the lakeside Edwardian mansion called Hotel Ard na Sidhe. Price: €210-€270 per night. website: www.killarneyhotels.ie

Northwest:

In the Northwest, besides Rosapenna, you might try the luxurious Enniscoe House near Crossmolina. It's located between the great links of Carne and Enniscrone, and not too far from Strandhill and Sligo. Price: about €100 a night. website: www.enniscoe.com

Most first-timers go to the Southwest—and for good reason. Four of the top five courses are located here. Pictured here: Tralee.

Dublin:

The capital is full of great hotels. The Brooks, the Shelbourne, the Clarence, the Merrion, and the Westin, just to name a few. If you avoid rush hour traffic, you're 30 minutes from The Island, Portmarnock, and St. Anne's. The European Club is 90 minutes to the south.

Northern Ireland:

The Magherabuoy House Hotel looks like a decent place to stay. It puts you 20 minutes from the great links course at Portstewart, and two great links at Portrush. The links at Castlerock is about 40 minutes away. Price: about £100 per night. www.magherabuoy.co.uk

Your Own Castle Anywhere in Ireland:

If you want to find a cottage, manor house, or castle to rent for a week or more, contact Elegant Ireland. In the business for 20 years, they arrange exotic rentals with or without staff in some of the country's nicest estates. www.elegant.ie

10

33 Secrets of Having a Great Irish Golf Vacation

Secret #1: When to go

You certainly don't go to Ireland for the weather.

For one, the country is as far north as Newfoundland. And it's one of the windiest places on Earth. But because of the Atlantic Gulf Stream that passes nearby, the temperatures are warmer in Ireland than you'd expect for a country at this latitude. It rarely freezes, rarely snows, and you can generally play links golf year-round. Inland courses, on the other hand, get too wet in the winter.

January and February are the coldest months: temperatures typically range between 40 and 45 Fahrenheit.

In the summer, it's typically between 60 and 70. Rarely will you get a day above 80. One thing to keep in mind is the amount of daylight. Because Ireland is so far north, summer days give you light well past 10 pm. In the winter, however, it gets too dark to play golf around 4 pm. Then there's the rain…

It rains one out of every three days on average in Ireland, and two out of every three days in the Southwest. It rains considerably more on the west coast in general than it does on the east. In short, there's no way to avoid the rain in Ireland, so just be prepared to deal with it. It's not uncommon to start a round in the sun,

You can take a golf trip to Ireland any time of the year. Here's a boat sailing near Portstewart in early October.

finish in the sun, and have two rain showers in between.

When's the best time to go? I like September and October, because it's not as crowded. But any time of year is fine. Each month has its advantage. In the summer it's warmer and drier, but more crowded and often more expensive. Winters are cooler, but not unplayable, and you can typically have almost any golf course in the country to yourself.

Keep in mind: Many courses offer huge discounts (50% off or more) between November and March. A few courses close in the winter, however, such as Old Head and Tralee.

> ## Where the term "fore" comes from
>
> Before the 1850s, golfers used a ball that was leather on the outside, with geese feathers on the inside. Making these balls was labor-intensive and expensive. So caddies were often fined if they lost one. On holes where it might be difficult to spot a drive, one of the caddies in a group went ahead of the tee box to the area where a drive should land. This guy was called the "forecaddie." If a player hit a tee shot that was heading in the forecaddie's direction, the group yelled "forecaddie" to warn him. This was eventually shortened to "fore," which was easier to yell. This is one explanation at least... there are others.
>
> There are written records of the term being used as early as the 1850s.

Secret #2: What to wear

A few items of clothing are critical: fleece winter hat, Gortex rain suit (we found the brand Zero Restriction the best), and wet-weather gloves. You need one pair of really good waterproof shoes, and a spare pair in case these are still wet the next day. A turtleneck or zip-up fleece and long underwear are essential any time other than summer.

Secret #3: What to bring—and what to leave at home

Golf balls and clubs are much more expensive in Ireland than in the States—bring what you need from home. You can get gloves, tees, and a rain cover for your bag while you're there. I recommend you also bring a hairdryer (with Ireland power adapter) so you can dry shoes and clothes you might need to wear the next day. You can also ask at your hotel or B&B.

Secret #4: How to bend the tee-time rules

The official tee time and reservation policies of Ireland's best golf courses are getting increasingly bureaucratic. As one tour operator said in *The Irish Times*, "The screws are being turned in terms and conditions. That flies in the face of the biggest sales pitch of Ireland: the friendly and accommodating people. Sometimes we're paying in full, non-refundable, up to nine months in advance." My advice: Keep in mind that tee-time policies and other course details in this book come from the "official" course literature. I've found these rules don't mean much in the real world.

Irish "Course Secretaries" and other club officials take their jobs very seriously. But the folks working in the pro shops are much more easy-

Most links courses do not take you past the clubhouse between nines. Pictured here: Portmarnock.

going. Whenever possible, speak directly to someone in the pro shop. It's likely you'll get to play whenever there's available time—no matter what the "official rules" say.

Dooks Golf Club, for example, says guests can play only between 10 am and 1 pm and between 2:30 pm and 5 pm on weekends. But we showed up at 8 am and got in the queue with the regular members, who even gave us a scorecard since the pro shop was not yet open.

Secret #5: Be prepared for Nine-out... and Nine-back

On most links courses, forget the beer and chilidog after the ninth hole.

Most links courses are laid out in "nine-out and nine-back" fashion. This means the first nine holes take you away from the clubhouse... and the back nine bring you home, with no snack bar in between. Some of the great links courses do pass the clubhouse at the turn (Waterville comes to mind), and others do have a snack shop somewhere on the course (Ballybunion, for example).

The only place we saw a beer-cart girl was Doonbeg. As much as I'm against ruining the natural links experience, it was nice to have a cold Guinness mid-round.

Secret #6: Travel with a purpose

You can't see everything in Ireland on one trip, so don't try to cover too much ground. The best way to have a good golf trip is to pick one section of the country, and limit your time on the road. Particularly good are two-course destinations like Ballybunion, Portrush, Ballyliffin, and Rosapenna, where you can spend two nights and play two great courses without having to repack your bags. Also, consider playing the really great courses (anything in the top 15) two days in a row. The best links courses are so good, you'll love getting a second chance. Save the sightseeing for another trip.

Secret #7: The importance of a handicap

"What do you play off of?"

That's the question you'll hear every time you play with an Irishman.

They don't mean which tees do you play from… but rather, what's your handicap.

Keep in mind that the Irish handicap system is completely different than what we use in the States. There are no course ratings or slope numbers. This means a guy who plays at the local muni course can have the same handicap as a guy who regularly plays The European Club. But I guarantee a 10-handicapper at the European Club will beat the pants off a 10-handicap from the local muni course.

One more thing regarding handicaps: Most Irish golf books tell you to make sure you have an official USGA handicap card with you on your trip to Ireland. I've never heard of anyone at any course ask a player for this. Don't bother with it if you don't have one. If you don't already have an official handicap, simply use an internet site such as Yahoo! (http://golf.sports.yahoo.com/tracker) to get an approximate handicap before you go. And you'll really only need this if you plan to play with locals.

Secret #8: The best $200 you will spend

It will typically take you at least twice as long to drive than what you are used to at home. For example, if you have 60 miles to cover, it would typically take you about an hour in the United States. In Ireland, it will take you an hour and a half, minimum. Ireland has highways only around major cities.

The roads and road markings can be very confusing. And remember, the Irish drive on the left. Hire a driver and you'll enjoy more of your trip. You can rent a bus for up to 12 with reclining leather seats, TV, DVD, storage area for clubs. It will cost you about $400-$500 a day. But remember, you'll also be avoiding the costs of a minivan (or two), which would cost you about $200 per van per day. There are dozens of companies in Ireland that will arrange to take you around in high-end cars and buses. I contacted Kennedy Coaches, who quoted me a

I recommend you hire a driver for your trip—you'll be a lot more relaxed, and will avoid pulling off a stunt like this.

rate of €340 a day for four people in a Mercedes van, and €385 per day for 8-10 people in a Mercedes bus with tables and leather chairs. E-mail them at kennedycoaches@eircom.net. For other options, go to www.ireland.ie, click on "getting around," then "coaches."

Secret #9: Night golf

Ireland is between 50 and 55 degrees latitude. This means it's farther north than any U.S. state except Alaska. If you hop in a plane in Shannon and fly straight west, maintaining the same degree of latitude of around 53 degrees, you'll come very close to hitting Calgary. The point is, because Ireland is so far

north, the summer days are very long. I've started play as late as 7 pm and have finished 18 holes, no problem. But keep in mind that in the winter, it gets dark very early—around 4 pm.

Secret #10: How to bet like the Irish

The course starter will ask you if you are a "two-ball" or a "four-ball." He means, how many people are in

In the summer in Ireland you can begin a round of golf as late as 7 pm. Pictured here: Connemara.

your group. If you and a friend want to play with two Irish guys (to make up a "four-ball"), and want to place a little wager, the Irish typically play two-man teams of best ball.

You simply subtract the lowest handicap among the foursome from the other three players' handicaps, and use the hole rankings to figure out where each player gets strokes. For example, let's say you're playing with a 4 handicap, a 10 handicap, a 12 handicap, and 16 handicap. The 16 handicap would get a stroke on the 12 hardest holes (16-4=12). The 12 handicap would get a stroke on the 8 hardest holes. The 10 handicap would get a stroke on the 6 hardest holes.

Why you find railroad ties in bunkers

At The European Club and a handful of other links courses, bunkers are lined with railroad ties, or "sleepers," as the Irish call them. There's a little history behind their use…

You see, when golf was just beginning in Ireland and the U.K. in the late 1800s, links courses were almost always located near railway stations. That's the only way anyone could get there. So when the track had to be repaired, sleepers were discarded onto the nearby courses. There, they were put to use to fortify bunkers and burns. Unlike U.S. courses, where bunkers rarely hurt your score, a links trap will usually cost you at least one stroke. As European Club owner Pat Ruddy says, "Don't complain that they are unfair. They are not meant to be pleasure beaches."

My friend Kevin's approach on The European Club's 12th lodged in the bunker-side ties. He whiffed, then played out fine.

The Irish like match-play best ball (no carryovers), with one bet for the front nine, one bet for the back nine, and one bet for the total. Usually, it's a small amount… like €4 or less for each part of the bet. The Irish also like handicap-adjusted Stableford format for larger competitions.

Secret #11: Beware—the Irish like to hang out naked

In Ireland, nearly everyone showers after completing a round of golf. After a shower, the Irish like to take care of all of their cosmetic needs with droopy and flabby parts hanging out for all to see. If you like hanging out with naked men, you'll love it here.

After showers, everyone goes to the clubhouse for a meal and a few drinks. A few clubhouses require a jacket. Bring one just in case. Never wear your golf shoes into any clubhouse.

Secret #12: Save 15% on everything you buy

If you buy anything expensive, be sure to ask for your VAT refund form. VAT is a 15% "value added tax." As a foreigner you are exempt, if you are taking your stuff out of the country. Just ask at the register when you pay.

Secret #13: How to make sure you get on to almost any course

The Irish, as a general rule, don't get up early to play golf. Some courses even have early-bird discounts (before 8 am). If you arrive at a golf course at the crack of dawn, there's a very good chance you can be the first one off the tee. In fact, you'll probably be the first one in the parking lot.

Secret #14: The secret of staying warm and dry

In Ireland, only old and crippled people use golf carts, or "buggies" as they call them. I recommend you play the game as it's meant to be played in Ireland: walk whenever possible. It's warmer and drier in bad weather to walk rather than ride. No zipping and unzipping golf cart covers. No sitting in puddles. Walking gets the blood flowing. The wind becomes a personal challenge, rather than a nuisance, as it is when you're in a golf cart.

Most Irish don't carry their clubs, however. They use a pull cart, or "trolley" as they call it. You can rent a trolley at every course in Ireland, usually for no more than €4. Many Irish golfers over the age of 40

Walking Ireland's links could be the world's best diet program. I lost 10 pounds while eating more junk food than I've had in my entire life.

have their own battery-operated trolley, usually with a remote control.

Secret #15: The easiest way to stay in touch

If you are going to personally handle golf and hotel arrangements while in Ireland, rent a cell phone for the trip. I got one from www.telestial.com. It arrived before I left home, so it was ready to use as soon as we landed in Shannon. If you are going for more than two weeks, it's probably cheaper to buy a prepaid phone when you arrive.

Here's another phone secret: When in Ireland, call the tourist board toll-free (1-850-230-330) for room reservations, ferry details, and anything else you need help with. When making calls

Even in the smallest towns, everyone has a mobile phone and uses it to send text messages, because calls are so expensive.

within the country, you do not need the country code (353) and must dial "0" before the rest of the number.

Secret #16: How to avoid getting lost

Ireland's roads are a mess—poorly marked, narrow, and often jam-packed. The best road map is produced by Ordnance Survey Ireland. You can order a copy before you leave home at: www.irishmaps.ie. The complete road atlas is just €12.50. You can also get a copy once you arrive.

Secret #17: How to slash the price of a rental car

If you must rent a car, prepay before you leave. You can save even more by using a credit card that has international car rental insurance. When I traveled, only certain MasterCards offered this option. To find one that still does, go to: www.mastercard.com. Ask specifically about car insurance in Ireland. Get as big a car as you can afford (Irish cars are smaller than comparable American versions), and get a manual transmission, which is much cheaper than an automatic.

Secret #18: How Irish golf rules are different from ours

The Irish are sticklers for golf's rules. This means no mulligans… no gimmees outside of a few inches… play the ball as it lies… don't ground your club in a hazard… and hit a provisional ball whenever necessary. If you don't normally play by the real rules of golf, learn to do so if you plan to play with locals.

Secret #19: Cheap calls from the United States

You can make most of your arrangements on-line, but if you need to call Ireland, I found a cheap way to do it. First dial 10-10-834. You must pay a 39-cent connection charge, but still, you can make a dozen calls for less than $10. For more details, go to: www.accerispartners.com and click on "residential products," where you'll find all the details.

Secret #20: A mathematical formula you need to know

Some courses are marked in yards… others in meters. Ask, if it's not written on the scorecard. A rough way to figure out meters-to-yards is to just add

Narin & Portnoo—one of the great undiscovered gems and bargains of Irish links golf.

10%. The real conversion is 1 meter equals 1.093 yards. So if the course markings say you are 150 meters, you're about 165 yards—163.95 exactly.

Also, a few of the great links courses, like Portstewart and Portrush, don't have any markings at all on some holes. Splurge for the yardage book or caddie.

Secret #21: The best travel guide book

For general travel information I like Lonely Planet guidebooks—a good mix of history and insight, with accommodation options for all budgets.

Secret #22: How to knock 5 strokes off your score

Splurge for a caddie as often as you can afford it. Several benefits: 1) you'll play better, 2) you'll lose fewer balls, 3) you'll enjoy walking the course while someone else carries your bag, and 4) you'll hear great stories. When making tee times, always tell the course in advance that you want a caddie. Share one caddie for two players to save money.

Secret #23: The secret to having fun no matter how you play

You will post some big numbers on links courses, especially if you play in bad weather. If you watch the British Open, you know what I mean, and most of the really hard courses in Ireland are more severe and dramatic than the courses in the rotation for the British Open. For this reason, match play is a

Photo: Mary Pat Fannon

The famous Giant's Causeway in Northern Ireland, near the links of Portstewart and Portrush.

great game. If you are having a bad round, you can spend all day looking for lost balls in the rough. Plus, match play encourages you to take chances, to go for the great shots that are most rewarding and most memorable.

Secret #24: How to know what the Irish are thinking and talking about

Gerry Ryan is Ireland's best morning radio talk-show host. If you want to know what the Irish are talking about, tune him in. People of all generations listen and call in. Gerry is on 2FM every weekday from 9 am to noon. You can listen on-line at: www.rte.ie/2fm/ryanshow/index2.html. One thing that's nice about Ireland is that you get the same radio stations throughout the entire country.

Secret #25: How to choose the right club

Links turf is different than the ground you're used to playing on. The lies are tighter, and the ball rolls a lot more than you're used to. It's almost always better to land the ball short of the green than it is to go long. Nine times out of 10 you will do better by taking too little club rather than too much. If you miss with too much club, the extra bounce can put you in really bad shape, especially if you miss right or left. We learned this the hard way.

Secret #26: How to save 50% or more on Ireland's top courses

Remember, you can play most of Ireland's links year-round. Travel November through March and you will not only have the courses to yourself, you'll save as much as 50% on some of the best links courses in the country. Another little trick: Many Irish courses give spouses playing together a 20% discount. Ask in the pro shop.

Secret #27: Secret passages that cut hours from your driving time

There are several ferries in Ireland that can shave hours of driving time. When traveling from Ballybunion to Lahinch and Doonbeg, for example, take the Shannon Ferry, instead of driving around the river (www.shannon-ferries.com).When traveling from Ballyliffin to Portstewart and Portrush, take the Lough Foyle Ferry (www.loughfoyleferry.com).

Secret #28: Have someone else handle all the details

There are literally dozens of tour companies that will handle all of the travel details for you, including airfare, ground transportation, tee times, and hotels. Some of the most well known groups are:

· PerryGolf (www.perrygolf.com)
· Adventures in Golf (www.adventures-in-golf.com)
· Jerry Quinlan's Celtic Golf (www.jqcelticgolf.com)
· Swing Golf Ireland (southwest tours only; www.swinggolfireland.com)
· JD Golf Tours (www.jdgolf.ie)
· Carr Golf (www.carrgolf.com)

This is a small sampling some of the most well-known firms. A five-minute web search will give you many more options.

Secret #29: How to cut your driving time by 75% or more—take a helicopter

Several private helicopter firms will cart you around the country, so you can avoid the terrible roads. Some copters fit four people and clubs, while others will hold eight and equipment. Prices start around €1,200 per flying hour. When I talked to the guy who runs Gaelic Helicopters, he told me if you want to fly into Shannon, for example, and take a helicopter to Waterville (normally a three and a half hour drive), it would cost around €2,500.

Dublin's famous Ha'Penny Bridge. There was a half-penny charge to cross the all-iron bridge (built in 1816) before 1919.

That's because you have to pay for the flight to pick you up, drop you off, and return to base in County Cork.

· Links Helicopters (www.linkshelicpoters.com)
· Gaelic Helicopters (www.gaelichelicopters.com)
· Blue Star (www.helicopters.ie)

Secret #30: Where to find your own piece of the Emerald Isle

If you want to own a piece of Ireland, or escape the rat race for several months, avoid Irish cities, and look to the countryside and small towns instead. As my colleague (and Irish resident) Steenie Harvey says: "Although Irish cities have become as frenetic and traffic-clogged as cities the world over, the country- side remains the

Portsalon in County Donegal—easily the best bargain in Irish links golf.

same as when I moved here: quiet... peaceful... safe." If you want to be near great links golf courses, try counties Clare, Kerry, Sligo, Donegal, and Antrim for starters.

Secret #31: The 10 best bargains in Irish links golf

These courses are not necessarily the cheapest in the country, but each course listed below gives you a great round of golf—world class, by any measure   for $90 or less. Often much less. Prices listed are weekday rates, unless otherwise noted. At the time of publication, €1 equaled $1.21, and £1 equaled $1.77.

1) Portsalon (€35)	6) Carne (€55 all the time)
2) Enniscrone (€50)	7) Donegal (€55)
3) Portrush (Valley; £35)	8) Rosapenna (Old; €50)
4) Narin & Portnoo (€30)	9) Rosapenna (Sandy Hills; €75)
5) Ardglass (£32)	10) Ballyliffin (Old; €60)

Honorable mention: Strandhill, Portstewart, Rosslare, St. Anne's, Laytown & Bettystown.

Secret #32: The five most overpriced links courses in Ireland

Again, not necessarily the most expensive courses in the country, but places where the quality of the golf does not justify the expense. Prices are weekend rates, unless otherwise noted. At the time of publication, €1 equaled $1.21, and £1 equaled $1.77.

1) Royal Dublin (€120)
2) Portmarnock Hotel & Golf Links (€125 all the time)
3) Baltray, County Louth (€130)
4) Portmarnock Old (€190)
5) Doonbeg (€195)

Secret #33: Undiscovered gems: The 10 best courses you've probably never heard of.

The links of Ireland are no longer a secret. Roughly 250,000 foreigners visit every year, primarily to play the country's links courses. However, there are still a few undiscovered gems... places the masses haven't yet caught onto. At several of these places, you are likely to be the only foreigner on the links on any given day...

1) Portsalon
2) Rosapenna (Sandy Hills)
3) Enniscrone
4) Ballyliffin (Glashedy)
5) Carne
6) Doonbeg
7) Narin & Portnoo
8) Ardglass
9) Laytown & Bettystown
10) Strandhill

11

Confessions of a Links Addict

By Pat Ruddy, Sr.

AUTHOR'S NOTE: Pat Ruddy is the best links golf architect in the world today. He loves the game in its original form—on the links. Mr. Ruddy is a throwback to an earlier generation, creating his designs by simply walking the land. No need for 3-D imaging. No aerial photos. Mr. Ruddy doesn't even have a website. Yet he has designed two of Ireland's Top-10 links from scratch, and has redesigned four others. Here are a few of his thoughts on what makes links golf so good, and how he goes about building a links course.

Photo courtesy of The European Club

Former newspaperman Pat Ruddy is now the best links golf architect in the world.

W hen I was a boy, there were many days when I was "too sick" to go to school.

On these mornings, when I couldn't face Latin verbs and algebraic conundrums, I strapped a few golf clubs to my bicycle's crossbar, slung a bag (stuffed with sandwiches and a flask of tea) over my shoulder, and pedaled 20 miles.

My destination: the great Rosses Point, a links golf course in Co. Sligo.

In school I never did see the use of trying to have A+B make a C, but I always enjoyed the flight of a well-struck mashie! At Rosses Point I hit hundreds of golf shots, found a game with kindred spirits, and had picnics in the long grasses watching the clouds scud by over Drumcliff Bay and Ben Bulben Mountain.

Even as a boy, I knew there was something entrancing, bewitching almost, about true links golf.

Most golfers don't understand the true meaning of links land. It is defined simply as "the sand deposits left behind by the receding oceans or blown up from the beaches, which form a link between the sterile seashore and the rich inland soils."

217

Despite what modern promoters of cliff-top golf would like to have you believe, it is only on this type of true links land that real links golf can be played.

The game of golf was invented on links land. It is where the game was always meant to be played. Once you leave the links, everything is a toned-down copy of the original.

Ruddy has built three new links (including The European Club, pictured here), and has redesigned four others.

Think about it. Mounds on today's modern courses simulate the dunes of the original links. Sand traps mimic the great sandpits of the old links. And lakes and ponds are there to replicate the sea!

Links golf is the beginning of the species. It is where the principles of the game were established. Down by the seaside in the wind and the rains and the dunes, with the rest of the world blocked out.

This is where golf goes on all year no matter what the weather. It is where the real golfing purist retreats to when it's time to restore the golfing soul. Golf on links land is a rare experience and should be cherished by those privileged to play it.

Now, almost 50 years have passed since my first links experience. It is a source of wonder to me that my life has retained such a strong connection with the dunes land.

How to build a links course

I have built my own fine links (if I may say so myself) at The European Club. In short, I have devoted nigh on 20 years of thought, labor, and capital to The European Club. In addition, I have been entrusted with the complete construction of two new links (one at Ballyliffin, the other at Rosapenna), plus extensive remodeling of older links at Rosapenna, Ballyliffin, Portsalon, and Donegal.

My design and redesign strategy is simple.

I like to combine the knowledge of the evolved game—knowing how much it has changed since the original classics were built—with imagination and the use of modern machinery. My aim is to produce a form of links golf that is fit to face the modern champion, and those of the next 50 years at least.

For the renovations I've worked on, my main task has been to minimize blind shots, to scale the challenge to golf's new technologies and the athleticism of today's game, and to order each links as a piece of great music, with ebbs and flows that build to a crescendo.

My goal is always to produce a landscape so beautiful that when players arrive they enjoy the nearest thing possible to a walk in golf's Garden of Eden. Because that is what golf is. A test of sinew, nerve, temperament and skill, and at the same time a soothing and elevating part of your existence.

It has been a privilege to work on links new and old. Even in my wildest dreams as a kid (when I was creating golf course plans on the back of my notebooks, signed by "Pat Ruddy, Master Golfer"), never did I put myself on the same design ticket as Old Tom Morris, Harry Vardon, and James Braid.

All three of these men worked on Rosapenna's great links in County Donegal. And it is here that I was allowed the privilege to build a new back nine for the 1890s links.

The old nine ran tamely inland, presumably to avoid engineering difficulties that were impossible to work around 100 years ago.

Photo courtesy of The European Club

Golf Magazine *ranks three of The European Club's holes among the top 500 in the world.*

I remember lying awake at night while working on Rosapenna, peering through the dark in the direction of the ceiling (which is always part of my process for building new golf holes). It became spooky. I half expected to see the faces of the three great old champions peering down at me. Would they smile approval or scowl at an interloper?

Through every move I kept these men in mind. And I took great care to resist all urgings to tamper with the lovely old holes on the front nine. Even 100 years later it remains a fine collection of undisturbed historic classics. I didn't move a single blade of grass.

I took similar care at nearby Portsalon, a links that was also founded in the 1890s. But here I had to cut deeper, as the course had become dangerous for modern play, with several criss-cross fairways and blind greens. We created 10 new holes to modern scale, and revised others so that Portsalon now measures about 7,000 yards. The course now stands in favorable comparison to the other great Irish links. (Mr. Palmer says it's one of the 10 best in Ireland.)

Similarly at Donegal I enjoyed the opportunity to work on the old Eddie Hackett layout. We built new greens at numbers 1, 2, 4, 9, 12, 13, 14, and 18. We redesigned many fairway features throughout. The results have pleased the club enough to see our association run over almost a decade.

I was able to stretch my creative muscle more freely at the three brand-new links I have created from scratch: the new links at Rosapenna, the new links at Ballyliffin, and my own beloved project at The European Club.

What a thrill it was to go to Ballyliffin with my late friend and Walker Cup player Tom Craddock. We were invited to have a look at the bunkers of the Old Course. But when we saw the spectacular surrounding land, we told the club and the township of about 800 souls to forget about fixing the old links for the moment, and to consider instead building a great new second course.

This was the early 1990s. I knew from my experience at The European Club that big changes were already afoot in Ireland. If the folks in Ballyliffin hadn't acted quickly, environmental and planning restrictions would have sterilized the use of the magnificent property. It was a great day when the town decided to go for it!

From my work at The European Club, I knew how to stretch a limited budget a long way through simple hard work. It paid off. The new links at Ballyliffin is now ranked among the top 60 courses in Britain and Ireland.

Why I built some holes in the middle of the night

The excitement associated with being a links builder in Ireland, where large budgets are reserved only for a few super-commercial developments, is difficult to describe. But let me give you an example, by telling you about how we built the 14th hole at Ballyliffin.

This hole came to life amid considerable local controversy. It was to be built into the side of a huge, white, blown-out dune, which some members wanted to preserve. They failed to realize that we needed to remodel the dune to make space. Plus, it was a wonderful location for a par-3, and the dune's blowing sand, if left unchecked, would simply submerge fairways and nearby greens.

We debated back and forth for several months. The discussions went nowhere. So I got permission from a few brave committee members to go out one winter's night and build the hole in the shroud of darkness.

It snowed and rained all night. Bitter cold, even in the cab of my excavator. But by dawn, with the help of a bulldozer operator and a truck driver, we had produced 90% of a magnificent new golf hole.

We waited anxiously in the early morning light, expecting hordes of distraught members to come defend what was left of the hill—and to perhaps even club me to death! But no one braved the weather that day… or the next. And when they did finally emerge it was only to express admiration for

Photo courtesy of The European Club

What's amazing is that Ruddy builds his courses simply by walking the land. No tech gadgets necessary.

221

what we had made.

I doubt if Jack, Arnie, Pete, or Greg have ever considered this approach.

We endured similar thrills and stresses as we built the links of The European Club. My wife, Bernardine, and teenage son, Gerry, joined with me in round-the-clock work and worries. I'm sure no other designer's wife has spent so many hours on her knees weeding young greens.

The work simply had to be done to ensure the financial future of our family. Our links required major investments, especially for a family of modest means.

Simply put, we risked everything to build what we thought was a great golf course, with the hopes that the golfers would come. And come they have.

The European Club has twice been voted into the top 100 courses in the world. The future, finally, seems safe. And the time has come for me to actually play golf, rather than drive earthmovers. This was, after all, the objective from the start.

We were certainly never in it for the money. Only a madman would risk his entire life savings in an attempt to get rich by building a golf course next to the sea, in a low population zone.

Golf in Ireland, of course, has changed dramatically during my lifetime. The links land of Ireland has become the summer magnet for hundreds of thousands of traveling golfers from Sweden, Finland, Germany, France, Britain, Canada, the United States, Africa, Asia, and Australia. The word is out that this is a great place to visit. The golf is marvelous and the welcome is unlike any other you will receive anywhere in the world.

Keep in mind, there is not a single golf club in Ireland that requires a member's introduction or sophisticated nurturing of friendships and net-working to secure a game.

After all, it is only a game, and the Irish have kept that in perspective even as golf has become a "product" to so many others.

You know, there's an old joke in Ireland. Whenever Irish golfers get together and discuss the possibility of reincarnation, there's always one fellow who wishes to return as a rabbit on one of the country's great golf links. As the explanation usually goes, there could hardly be a nicer prospect than making love, lying about in the sun, and watching links golf all day.

My country's combination of superbly primeval golfing lands, and a warm-hearted bunch of people, makes a golf trip to Ireland mandatory for anyone who loves the game and wants to get in touch with the game's origins. It is a fact that nearly one third of the world's 160-or-so true links are squeezed onto this tiny island, where golf is played all year round, thanks to the warming effect of the Gulf Stream.

In fact I think a name change is in order. From The Emerald Isle and the Island of Saints & Scholars, I like to think of it today as the most remarkable Island of Golf. Be assured of a *Cead Mile Failte* (a hundred thousand welcomes).

— Pat Ruddy
The European Club
December 2005

Pat Ruddy's Top 20 Links in Ireland

Only in Ireland would the country's top golf course designer reply to an unsolicited letter from a guy he's never heard of on the other side of the world. But that's exactly what Pat Ruddy did when I contacted him about writing a chapter for my book. When I asked Mr. Ruddy to name his top 10 links courses in Ireland, he hesitated, but finally gave in. Here's what he wrote:

"You ask would I name my ten FAVOURITE Irish links? Dangerous. So little between many of them for enjoyment. However, if you allow me 20 FAVOURITES, so that people would not wonder how I left out so-and-so (they not knowing that these are hair's-breadth judgments), here we go in the order of my choice… and bedamned if people think I am biased in my first choice, because I just may be that! Best regards and may the Lord have mercy on me should you publish this list…"

1. The European Club
2. Rosapenna (Sandy Hills)
3. Ballyliffin (Glashedy)
4. Waterville
5. County Louth (Baltray)
6. Donegal (Murvagh)
7. Royal County Down
8. Portmarnock
9. Portsalon
10. County Sligo
11. Royal Dublin
12. Lahinch
13. Ballybunion (Old)
14. Royal Portrush
15. Tralee
16. The Island
17. Ballybunion (Cashen)
18. Portstewart
19. Carne
20. Connemara

12

Ratings From Other Golf Publications

Y ou might also like to see how other publications rank the links courses of Ireland. Keep in mind: All of these rankings include both parkland and links courses. And remember, these rankings were most likely put together by a group of people, none of whom have actually played every course in the country. Take *Golf Digest's* rankings, below, for example. No one in his right mind who has played both The European Club and County Louth Golf Club would ever put these courses on the same page, much less rank County Louth higher.

Ireland's Top 20 from *Golf Digest,* November, 2003

1. Royal Portrush (Dunluce)
2. Royal County Down
3. Portmarnock
4. Ballybunion (Old)
5. Lahinch
6. Waterville
7. County Louth
8. Sligo
9. The European Club
10. Carne
11. The K Club (North)
12. Mount Juliet
13. Doonbeg
14. Portstewart (Strand)
15. Headfort (New)
16. Old Head
17. Druid's Glen
18. Killarney
19. Enniscrone
20. Adare Manor

Irish Links that Made it into *Golf Magazine's* Top 100 2003 Worldwide Courses

#10. Royal County Down
#12. Royal Portrush (Dunluce Links)
#13. Ballybunion (Old)
#40. Portmarnock
#73. Lahinch
#98. The European Club

Barron's Top 10 Courses in Ireland (links only)

1. Waterville
2. Royal Portrush (Dunluce)
3. Ballybunion (Old)
4. Portmarnock
5. The European Club
6. Lahinch
7. Royal County Down
8. Portstewart
9. Sligo
10. Ballyliffin (Glashedy)

Golf Digest, May 2005, Irish Rankings

Republic of Ireland

1. Ballybunion (Old)
2. Lahinch
3. Portmarnock
4. The European Club
5. Waterville
6. County Sligo
7. Mount Juliet
8. Royal Dublin
9. Druid's Glen
10. Carton House (Montgomerie)
11. Adare Manor
12. Carne
13. County Louth
14. Doonbeg
15. Cork
16. Headfort (New)
17. The Island
18. Carlow
19. Dromoland Castle
20. Enniscrone

Northern Ireland

1. Royal Portrush (Dunluce)
2. Royal County Down
3. Portstewart
4. Clandeboye
5. Malone

Even middle-rung links courses have spectacular seaside holes. Here's one of Strandhill's, ranked 30th overall.

13

Sources

This book would have been impossible without the excellent pre-existing books and magazine articles on Irish golf. These books were the original sources for many of the stories, facts, and anecdotes in *Secrets of the Irish Links*. From the list below, I particularly recommend *Links of Heaven, Golfing in Ireland, Links Golf The Inside Story, The Greatest Game Ever Played*, and *The Making of the Celtic Tiger*, which I've marked with an asterisk (*).

BOOKS, MAGAZINES, and NEWSPAPER ARTICLES

* Armstrong, Rob, *Golfing in Ireland*, Gretna, LA, Pelican Publishing, 1997.

* Daley, Paul, *Links Golf The Inside Story*, Gretna, LA, Pelican Publishing, 2001.

Doak, Tom, *The Confidential Guide to Golf Courses,* Chelsea, MI, Sleeping Bear, 1996.

Dwyre, Bill, "It's an Irish Spectacle," *The Los Angeles Times*, July 17, 2003.

Frick, Robert, "Playing of the Green," *Kiplinger's Personal Finance*, July 2005.

Frost, Mark, *The Greatest Game Ever Played*, New York, NY, Hyperion, 2002.

Holland, Charles Hepworth, *The Irish Landscape*, Edinburgh, Dunedin Academic Press, 2003.

Lonely Planet Ireland, 2004.

Lynch, Eamon, "The Man Who Said 'No' to Augusta—20 Times!" *Golf Magazine*, April, 2005.

* Mac Sharry, Ray & Padraic White, *The Making of the Celtic Tiger: The inside story of Ireland's economic boom*, Mercier Press, 2001.

Morris, Jan, "Ireland Shiny, Brash and Confident," *The New York Times Magazine*, November 21, 2004.

Morris, Jan, *Pleasures of a Tangled Life*, New York, Vintage Books, 1989.

Peet, John, "The Luck of the Irish," *The Economist*, October 16th, 2004.

* Phinney, Richard & Scott Whitley, *Links of Heaven*, Ogdensburg, NY, Baltray Books, 1996.

* Redmond, John, *The Book of Irish Golf*, Gretna, LA, Pelican Publishing, 1997.

Shackelford, Geoff, *Grounds for Golf—The history and fundamentals of golf course design*, New York, St. Martin's Press, 2003.

Shackelford, Geoff, "Links: Where the Turf Mimics the Surf," *Los Angeles Times*, July 17, 2003.

Simpson, Glenn, "Irish Subsidy Lets Microsoft Slash Taxes in U.S. and Europe," *The Wall Street Journal*, November 7, 2005.

Taddeo, Lisa, "It Takes a Village," *Golf Magazine*, November, 2005.

Wert, William, "Ireland's Greens," *Barron's*, October 18, 1999.

Williams, Tom, *Fairways of the Sea—100 Years of Golf at Rosslare 1905 – 2005*.

WEBSITES

www.irishgolf.com: From the authors of *Links of Heaven*, this is easily the best website on everything related to Irish golf. Here you'll find links to every individual course, tour operators, and much, much more.

About the Author

Michael Palmer grew up playing municipal golf courses in Baltimore (Maryland, not County Cork). He has been in publishing for more than a decade. The first half of this time was spent at a travel magazine called *International Living*. His articles have appeared in more than a dozen publications, including *Golf Digest*. Palmer has traveled extensively around the globe and has twice resided in Ireland—in Limerick and Waterford. Today he is an advertising copywriter for an investment research publishing firm in Baltimore, where he resides with his wife and daughter.